The Freshwater Angler™

AMERICA'S FAVORITE
Fish Recipes

CREATIVE
PUBLISHING
international

MINNETONKA, MINNESOTA

President/CEO: David D. Murphy

AMERICA'S FAVORITE FISH RECIPES

Authors and Project Directors: Peggy Ramette, Dick Sternberg
Editor: Janice Cauley
Project Manager: Joseph Cella
Senior Art Director: Bradley Springer
Art Director: Dave Schelitzche
Home Economists: Ellen Meis, Peggy Ramette, Grace Wells
Dietitian: Hill Nutrition Associates, Inc.
Research Director: Eric Lindberg
Researchers: Steven Hauge, Mike Hehner, Jim Moynagh
Director of Development Planning & Production: Jim Bindas
Photo Studio Manager: Cathleen Shannon
Lead Photographers: Mette Nielsen, Mike Parker
Staff Photographers: Rex Irmen, John Lauenstein, Bill Lindner,
  Mark Macemon, Paul Najlis
Photo Staff: Adam Esco, Melissa Grabanski, Eva Hanson,
  Paul Najlis, Rena Tassone
Contributing Photographers: Phil Aarestad, Linda Glantz,
  Chuck Nields
Styling Director: Bobbette Destiche
Food Stylists: Darcy Gorris, Nancy Johnson
Contributing Food Stylists: Sue Brue, Sue Finley, Carol Grones,
  Melinda Hutchison
Production Manager: Amelia Merz
Production Staff: Diane Dreon-Krattiger, Joe Fahey, Jeff Hickman,
  Mike Schauer, Linda Schloegel, Nik Wogstad
Shop Staff: Jim Huntley, Phil Juntti, Greg Wallace

Contributors: Dr. Paul Addis/University of Minnesota; Louis
  Bignami; Coleman Outdoor Products, Inc.; Buzz Ramsey/Luhr
  Jensen & Sons, Inc.; Normark Corporation; Robert E. Rust/Iowa
  State University; Jim Schneider

Printed on American paper by: R. R. Donnelley & Sons Co.
10 9 8 7 6 5 4 3 2

Library of Congress
Cataloging-in-Publication Data

Ramette, Peggy L.
America's favorite fish recipes / by Peggy L. Ramette
and Dick Sternberg
p. cm. – (The Hunting & fishing library)
Includes index.
ISBN 0-86573-039-3 (hardcover)
1. Cookery (Fish) I. Sternberg, Dick. II. Title.
III. Series.
TX747.R365 1992   92-6416
641.6'92 – dc20

Books available from the publisher: *The Art of Freshwater Fishing, The New Cleaning & Cooking Fish, Fishing With Live Bait, Largemouth Bass, Panfish, The Complete Guide to Hunting, Fishing With Artificial Lures, Successful Walleye Fishing, Smallmouth Bass, Dressing & Cooking Wild Game, Freshwater Gamefish of North America, Trout, Fishing Rivers & Streams, Fishing Tips & Tricks, White-tailed Deer, Northern Pike & Muskie, The Art of Fly Tying, America's Favorite Wild Game Recipes, Advanced Bass Fishing, Upland Game Birds, North American Game Animals, North American Game Birds, Advanced Whitetail Hunting, Understanding Whitetails, Fly-Fishing Equipment & Skills, Fishing Nymphs, Wet Flies & Streamers, Fly-Tying Techniques & Patterns, Fishing Dry Flies, Bowhunting Equipment & Skills, Wild Turkey, Muzzleloading, Duck Hunting, Venison Cookery, Game Bird Cookery, Fly Fishing for Trout in Streams, Fishing for Catfish, Modern Methods of Ice Fishing*

Contents

Introduction

All-time Favorite Fish Recipes is just that – a compilation of North America's best fish recipes. We've even tossed in a few European favorites.

To collect a wide selection of recipes, we invited our readers to submit their top personal choices. We tapped the brains of our own staff to recall great dishes they had run across in their travels; then we contacted the particular lodges and restaurants to get the details. We also invited well-known outdoor writers to send us their prized recipes.

Then our home economists chose the best of the best. All dishes were sampled by staff members and other anglers to make sure they passed the taste test.

Each section of the book covers a different fish-preparation technique, from campfire cooking to oven frying to pickling. We give you the basic information on each technique, followed by a selection of recipes using that method.

If a recipe calls for a species of fish you don't have, refer to the substitution chart on page 6 for an alternate choice.

This book also presents handy fish-cleaning tips, like how to reduce contaminants and improve flavor. For a complete guide to fish-cleaning techniques, refer to

Cleaning & Cooking Fish, published by The Hunting & Fishing Library®.

Nutritional information and exchanges for weight loss follow each recipe. When a recipe serves four to six persons, the data applies to the greater number of servings. In the case of alternate ingredients, that analysis applies to the first ingredient listed; optional ingredients are not included. Analyses of recipes that call for "any freshwater fish" were done with walleyes. Other species information is based on USDA figures.

Many fishermen think the only good way to cook fish is to fry them. For something different, they might try a new type of breading. The remarkable variety of recipes in this book opens up a whole new world of freshwater fish cookery.

Substitution Chart

If you don't have the kind of fish specified in a recipe, use this chart to find a replacement. The fish are categorized by size and oil content, the two most important factors in determining a good substitute.

Find the specified fish in the chart, then select any other fish in the same category. For example, if a recipe calls for walleye, substitute largemouth bass, northern pike, or any other fish in the large lean category.

LARGE OILY FISH (2 lbs. and larger)	COMMON NAMES
Salmon	
Chinook	King salmon, spring salmon, tyee
Coho	Silver salmon, blueback
Sockeye	Red salmon, blueback salmon
Pink	Humpback salmon, humpy, autumn salmon
Chum	Dog salmon, calico salmon
Atlantic	Landlocked salmon, Sebago salmon
Lake Trout	Laker, mackinaw, gray trout, togue
Brook Trout	Eastern brook trout, brookie, speckled trout, squaretail
Brown Trout	German brown, Loch Leven trout, brownie
Rainbow Trout	Bow, red-band trout, silver trout, steelhead, Kamloops
Cutthroat Trout	Native trout, cut, red throat, mountain trout

SMALL OILY FISH (up to 2 lbs.)	COMMON NAMES
Salmon	
Kokanee	Sockeye, red salmon
Stream Trout	
Brook	Eastern brook trout, brookie, speckled trout, squaretail
Brown	German brown, Loch Leven trout, brownie
Rainbow	Bow, red-band trout, silver trout, steelhead, Kamloops
Cutthroat	Native trout, cut, red throat, mountain trout
Whitefish	
Cisco	Tullibee, herring, lake herring
Mountain Whitefish	Whitefish, Rocky Mountain whitefish
Lake Whitefish	Common whitefish, Great Lakes whitefish, Sault whitefish

LARGE LEAN FISH (2 lbs. and larger)	COMMON NAMES
Bass	
Largemouth	Black bass, green bass, bigmouth, linesides
Smallmouth	Bronzeback, brown bass, black bass, Oswego bass, green trout, redeye
Striped	Striper, rockfish, linesides
White	Silver bass, striper, sand bass
Walleye	Walleyed pike, pickerel, jackfish, doré
Sauger	Sand pike, river pike, gray pike, gray pickerel, spotfin pike, jackfish
Northern Pike	Great northern pike, jack, pickerel, snake, gator
Muskellunge	Muskie, lunge, maskinonge, great pike

SMALL LEAN FISH (up to 2 lbs.)	COMMON NAMES
Bass	
Largemouth	Black bass, green bass, bigmouth, linesides
Smallmouth	Bronzeback, brown bass, black bass, Oswego bass, green trout, redeye
White	Silver bass, striper, sand bass
Sunfish	
Bluegill	Sun perch, bream, copperbelly, roach
Pumpkinseed	Common sunfish, yellow sunfish, bream
Redear	Shellcracker, stumpknocker, bream
Crappie	Papermouth, speckled perch
Yellow Perch	Raccoon perch, ringed perch

CATFISH AND BULLHEADS	COMMON NAMES
Catfish	
Flathead	Mud cat, yellow cat, shovelhead cat
Channel	Spotted cat, blue channel cat, fiddlers
Blue	Forktail cat, great blue cat, silver cat
Bullhead	Horned pout

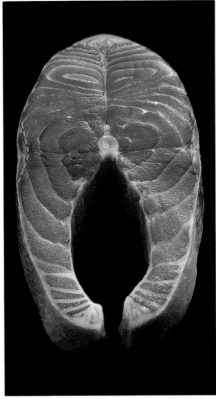

CUT AWAY any dark-colored meat along the sides of the fillets to remove any fat-soluable contaminants and improve the flavor. Also discard the back and belly meat if you suspect contaminants. The photo (left) shows exactly what meat to remove (dotted lines). If you skin your fillets (right), cut away the shallow band of dark meat along the lateral line, using an extremely sharp fillet knife. Remove the fatty tissue along the back and belly.

SPRINKLE table salt on your cleaning board to prevent the fish from sliding around. This way, you can clean the fish more easily and there's less risk of cutting yourself. Rinse the salt off your fish before cooking.

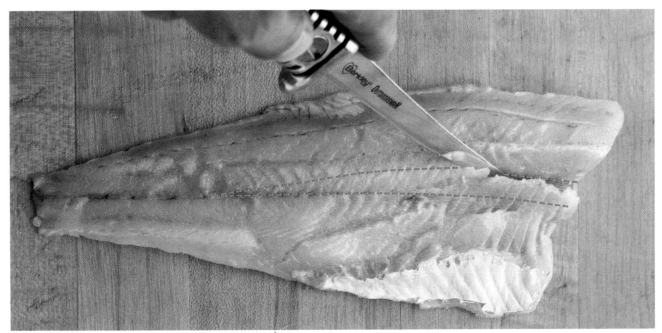

REMOVE the row of small bones that remains in the fillets of walleyes, largemouth bass and many other kinds of fish by cutting away a narrow strip of meat (dotted lines) just above the rib cage. You can easily locate the bone line by running your finger down the fillet before making your cuts.

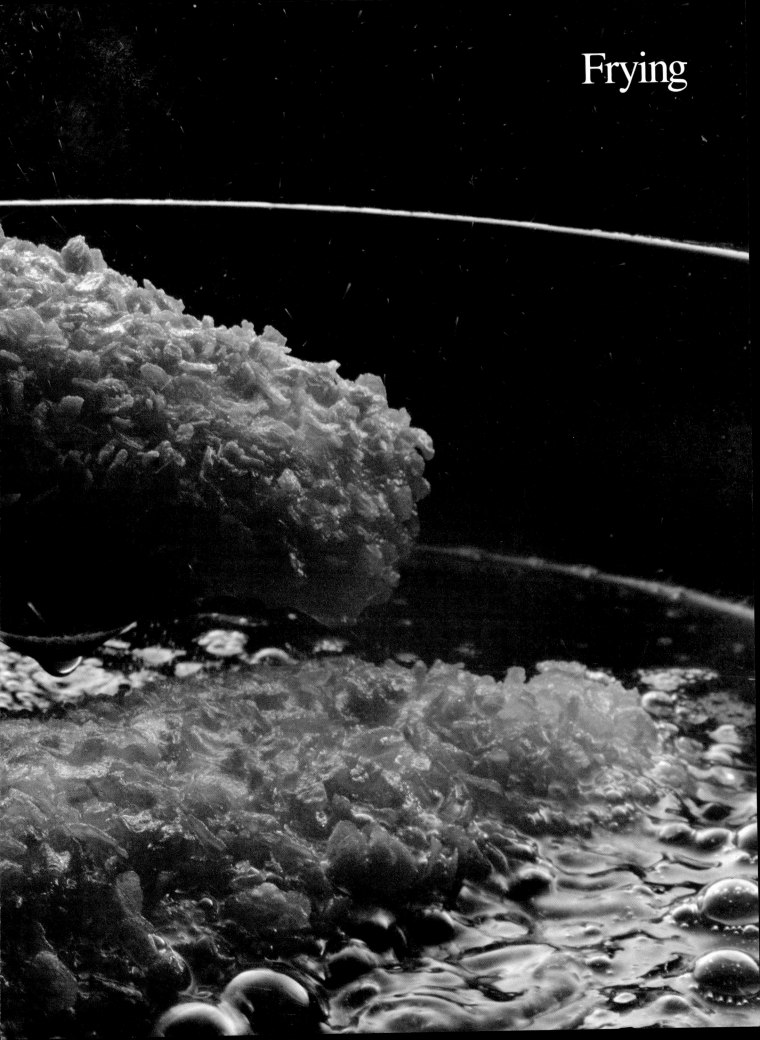

Frying

Techniques for Frying

One of the most popular fish-preparation techniques, frying, may be done in three different ways: pan-frying, stir-frying and deep-frying. The high cooking temperature (up to 375°F) seals in the juices and cooks the fish rapidly.

Fish with a low to moderate oil content work best for frying; oily fish are too rich.

PANFRYING. Fillets, steaks or small whole fish are fried in a large uncovered frying pan or electric skillet with a ⅛ to ½-inch layer of vegetable oil or a blend of butter or margarine and vegetable oil. Don't use pieces of fish that are more than 1½ inches thick.

Usually the fish are first dredged in flour, cornmeal, cracker crumbs, cornflake crumbs or a seasoned coating mix.

With some heavier types of coatings, such as cracker crumbs, the fish should first be dipped in beaten eggs to help the coating adhere, so it doesn't come off during the frying process.

STIR-FRYING. With this traditional Oriental method, bite-size pieces of fish are cooked in a wok or large frying pan with a mixture of vegetables in a sauce.

Hot vegetable or peanut oil is usually flavored with seasonings such as fresh gingerroot or garlic before the fish and vegetables are added.

Because the food is cooked over high heat, it must be stirred constantly to prevent burning. Always use firm-textured fish, so the stirring doesn't break up the pieces.

DEEP-FRYING. Fillets or small whole fish are first coated with a batter, then immersed in vegetable oil heated to 350 to 375°F. Use a deep-frying or candy thermometer to make sure the temperature stays in this range.

You can use a variety of batters, but make sure your batter is cold; otherwise, it will soak up too much oil. Dry the fish with paper towels before dipping, to ensure that the batter sticks to the fish.

Lower fish into the oil slowly, so the batter doesn't come off. It will form a crispy shell, keeping the fish moist but not greasy.

If you don't have a deep-fryer, simply use a heavy frying pan with sides at least 2 inches high, or a Dutch oven with about 1 to 2 inches of oil. When one side of the fish is done, turn to cook the other side.

FRYING EQUIPMENT for deep-frying includes (1) electric deep-fryer or (2) Dutch oven; (3) thermometer; (4) slotted spoon or (5) long-handled tongs for removing fish and (6) rack, for draining fish. For stir-frying, you'll need a (7) wok skillet or (8) wok. For panfrying, use a (9) heavy skillet with high sides and (10) spatula.

Tips for Frying Fish

TEST the oil to make sure it's hot enough by dropping in a small piece of bread or fish. It should brown in less than a minute. Don't test with water; it will pop and cause the hot oil to splatter.

AVOID deep-frying too many pieces of fish at once. The coated pieces will stick together, and the oil temperature will drop below 350°F, resulting in soggy fish.

KEEP deep-fried fish crispy by placing them on a wire rack over a paper-towel-lined plate. Keep them in a warm oven while frying another batch. If you put them on paper towels, the coating may not stay as crisp.

STRAIN cooled deep-frying oil so you can use it several times. Place a potato slice in the hot oil to remove off flavors, then strain cooled oil through a piece of cheesecloth. Store oil in sealed container in refrigerator.

Sautéed Trout → with Wild Mushrooms

John Holt – Whitefish, Montana

    4   cups cold water
  1/2   cup uncooked wild rice
 1 1/2 teaspoons olive oil
 2 1/2 oz. dried morel mushrooms
    2   cups hot water
  1/4   cup plus 1 tablespoon
        margarine or butter, divided
    4   whole drawn stream trout
        (8 oz. each)
        Salt
        Pepper
        Lemon wedges

4 servings

In 2-quart saucepan, combine water, rice and oil. Bring to a boil over medium-high heat, stirring occasionally. Cover. Reduce heat to low. Simmer for 30 minutes. Turn off heat. Let stand, covered, for 25 to 30 minutes, or until rice reaches desired consistency. Drain and discard water from rice. Cover to keep warm. Set aside.

Place mushrooms in medium mixing bowl. Pour hot water over mushrooms. Let soak for 30 minutes, or until softened. Drain and discard liquid. Set mushrooms aside.

In 12-inch skillet, melt 2 tablespoons margarine over medium heat. Add mushrooms. Cook for 4 to 5 minutes, or until lightly browned, stirring constantly. Remove mushrooms from skillet. Cover to keep warm. Set aside.

In same skillet, melt remaining 3 tablespoons margarine over medium heat. Add trout. Fry for 8 to 10 minutes, or until trout are golden brown and fish begins to flake when fork is inserted at backbone in thickest part of fish, turning over once. Remove from heat.

Spoon rice on serving platter. Arrange trout on rice. Sprinkle mushrooms evenly over fish and rice. Sprinkle evenly with salt and pepper to taste. Garnish with lemon wedges.

Per Serving: Calories: 422 • Protein: 32 g.
• Carbohydrate: 27 g. • Fat: 21 g.
• Cholesterol: 76 mg. • Sodium: 211 mg.
Exchanges: 1 starch, 3 1/2 lean meat,
2 vegetable, 2 fat

Trout Saussignac ↑

Frederick W. Montanye – Chateau de Saussignac Cooking School, Saussignac, France

2 tablespoons margarine or butter, divided
¼ cup chopped hazelnuts
2 whole drawn stream trout (8 oz. each)
2 tablespoons snipped fresh sorrel leaves
1 tablespoon vegetable oil
2 tablespoons snipped fresh parsley

2 servings

In 12-inch skillet, melt 1 tablespoon margarine over medium heat. Add hazelnuts. Cook for 1 to 2 minutes, or until lightly browned, stirring constantly. Place nuts in small bowl. Set aside.

Stuff cavity of each trout with 1 tablespoon sorrel. Wipe out skillet with paper towels. In same skillet, heat remaining 1 tablespoon margarine and the oil over medium heat until margarine is melted. Add trout. Fry for 6 to 8 minutes, or until trout are golden brown and fish begins to flake when fork is inserted at backbone in thickest part of fish, turning over once. Before serving, sprinkle evenly with nuts and parsley.

Per Serving: Calories: 413 • Protein: 30 g. • Carbohydrate: 3 g.
• Fat: 32 g. • Cholesterol: 76 mg. • Sodium: 172 mg.
Exchanges: 4 lean meat, ½ vegetable, 3½ fat

Salmon with Fresh Tomato & Basil

Elinor Klivans – Camden, Maine

3 tablespoons olive oil

4 salmon, or substitute, steaks
    (8 oz. each), 1 inch thick

1 cup coarsely chopped onions

2 cloves garlic, minced

1 tablespoon snipped fresh basil
    leaves

2 cups peeled seeded chopped
    tomatoes

¼ cup water

¼ teaspoon salt

¼ teaspoon freshly ground
    pepper

4 servings

In 10-inch skillet, heat oil over medium heat. Add steaks. Fry for 2 to 4 minutes, or until golden brown, turning over once. Remove steaks from skillet. Set aside.

To same skillet, add onions. Cook for 1 to 2 minutes, or until tender-crisp. Add garlic and basil. Cook for 1 minute. Stir in remaining ingredients.

Arrange steaks over tomato mixture. Reduce heat to low. Cover. Simmer for 11 to 13 minutes, or until fish is firm and opaque and just begins to flake. Serve over hot cooked linguine, if desired.

Per Serving: Calories: 410 • Protein: 41 g. • Carbohydrate: 8 g. • Fat: 23 g. • Cholesterol: 110 mg. • Sodium: 233 mg.
Exchanges: 5½ lean meat, 1½ vegetable, 1 fat

Bass Hemingway

Elisabeth A. Panelli – Reno, Nevada

2¼ lbs. bass, or substitute, fillets
   (6 oz. each), skin removed,
   cut in half crosswise
¼ cup grated Parmesan cheese
¼ teaspoon salt
¼ teaspoon pepper
1 cup all-purpose flour
¾ cup flat beer
1 tablespoon olive oil
1 tablespoon soy sauce
2 eggs, separated
1 teaspoon dry mustard
4 oz. Provolone cheese
4 oz. Muenster cheese
¼ cup snipped fresh parsley
¼ cup bacon drippings
¼ cup margarine or butter
   Lemon wedges

6 servings

Place fillets between 2 sheets of plastic wrap or wax paper. Pound gently with flat side of meat mallet to ¼-inch thickness. Remove top sheet of plastic wrap. Sprinkle top side of each fillet evenly with Parmesan, salt and pepper. Set aside.

In medium mixing bowl, beat together flour, beer, oil, soy sauce, egg yolks and mustard. Cover beer batter with plastic wrap. Chill.

Cut 12 thin strips each Provolone and Muenster cheese, each strip one-third width of fillets. Place 1 strip of each cheese on top of each fillet. Sprinkle evenly with parsley. Roll up each fillet; secure roll-ups with wooden picks. Set aside.

In medium mixing bowl, beat egg whites at high speed of electric mixer to soft peaks. Fold egg whites into beer batter.

In 12-inch skillet, heat bacon drippings and margarine over medium heat. Dip each roll-up in batter. Add to skillet. Fry for 10 to 13 minutes, or until all sides are deep golden brown, turning occasionally. Drain on paper-towel-lined plate.

Per Serving: Calories: 563 • Protein: 47 g. • Carbohydrate: 18 g. • Fat: 31 g. • Cholesterol: 224 mg. • Sodium: 834 mg. Exchanges: 1¼ starch, 6¼ medium-fat meat

Green Peppercorn & Raspberry Vinegar Bass ↑

Rudy Liebl III – Fresno, California

⅓ cup all-purpose flour
1½ lbs. bass, or substitute, fillets
   (6 oz. each), skin removed,
   cut in half crosswise
   Vegetable oil
1 tablespoon vegetable oil
¼ cup chopped shallots

½ cup ready-to-serve chicken broth
¼ cup crème de cassis
3 tablespoons raspberry vinegar
1 tablespoon fresh lemon juice
½ cup brown sauce*
2 tablespoons brined green
   peppercorns, drained

4 servings

Place flour in shallow dish. Dredge fillets in flour to coat. In 12-inch skillet, heat ⅛ inch oil over medium heat. Add fillets. Fry for 4 to 7 minutes, or until golden brown, turning over once. Remove fillets from skillet. Place on serving platter. Cover to keep warm. Set aside.

In 10-inch skillet, heat 1 tablespoon oil over medium heat. Add shallots. Cook for 1½ to 2 minutes, or until tender. Stir in broth, crème de cassis, vinegar and juice. Bring mixture to a simmer. Reduce heat to medium-low. Simmer for 10 to 15 minutes, or until mixture is reduced by half, stirring occasionally. Add brown sauce and peppercorns. Simmer for 1 minute, or until hot, stirring constantly. Spoon sauce over fish.

*Brown sauce may be purchased in specialty stores or in the Oriental section of your supermarket.

Per Serving: Calories: 546 • Protein: 34 g. • Carbohydrate: 40 g. • Fat: 24 g. • Cholesterol: 116 mg. • Sodium: 487 mg. Exchanges: ¾ starch, 4½ lean meat, ½ fruit, 2 fat

← Potato-flaked Fillets

"This is Mom's recipe with a few additions of my own."
Vern Downey – Maple Heights, Ohio

⅔ cup all-purpose flour
1 teaspoon paprika
¼ teaspoon salt
¼ teaspoon pepper
¼ teaspoon garlic powder
¼ teaspoon onion powder
2 eggs, beaten
2 cups instant potato buds or flakes
Vegetable oil
2¼ lbs. walleye, or substitute, fillets (6 oz. each), skin removed

6 servings

In shallow dish, combine flour, paprika, salt, pepper, garlic powder and onion powder. Place eggs in small mixing bowl. Place potato buds in second shallow dish. Dredge fillets first in flour mixture, then dip in eggs, and then dredge in potato buds to coat.

In 12-inch skillet, heat ¼ inch oil over medium heat. Add fillets. Fry for 4½ to 7 minutes, or until golden brown, turning over once. Drain on paper-towel-lined plate. Serve with lemon wedges and tartar sauce, if desired.

Per Serving: Calories: 450 • Protein: 37 g.
• Carbohydrate: 23 g. • Fat: 22 g.
• Cholesterol: 217 mg. • Sodium: 214 mg.
Exchanges: 1½ starch, 4½ lean meat, 1¾ fat

Potato & Onion Fried Bass

Roger D. Flanders – Gardnerville, Nevada

1½ lbs. bass, or substitute, fillets (6 oz. each), skin removed, cut in half crosswise
¼ teaspoon pepper
1½ cups instant potato buds or flakes
1 pkg. (1 oz.) dry onion soup mix
2 eggs, beaten
Vegetable oil

4 servings

Sprinkle fillets evenly with pepper. In food processor or blender, combine potato buds and soup mix. Process until mixture is powdery. Place mixture in shallow dish. Place eggs in medium mixing bowl. Dredge fillets first in potato mixture, then dip in eggs, and then dredge in potato mixture to coat.

In 12-inch skillet, heat ⅛ inch oil over medium heat. Add fillets. Fry for 3½ to 5½ minutes, or until golden brown, turning over once. Drain on paper-towel-lined plate.

Per Serving: Calories: 493 • Protein: 37 g. • Carbohydrate: 18 g. • Fat: 30 g.
• Cholesterol: 222 mg. • Sodium: 804 mg.
Exchanges: 1¼ starch, 4¾ lean meat, 3 fat

Gram Garsino's →
Garlic-fried Trout

Phyllis Garsino – Stockton, California

2¼ lbs. stream trout, walleye, or
    substitute, fillets (6 oz. each),
    skin removed
1   cup milk
1   cup seasoned dry bread crumbs
10 to 12 cloves garlic
¼   cup olive oil
¼   cup vegetable oil

6 servings

Arrange fillets in single layer in
13 × 9-inch baking dish. Pour milk
over fillets, turning to coat. Cover
with plastic wrap. Refrigerate 12
hours or overnight.

Place bread crumbs in shallow
dish. Drain and discard milk from
fillets. Dredge fillets in bread
crumbs to coat. Place coated fillets
on wax-paper-lined baking sheet.
Chill ½ hour.

Place each garlic clove under flat
side of wide-bladed knife. Strike
flat side of blade with heel of
hand to break cloves open.

In 12-inch skillet, heat oils and 5
or 6 cloves garlic over medium
heat. Add fillets. Fry for 7 to 9
minutes, or until golden brown,
turning over once and adding remaining cloves garlic after half
of cooking time. Drain on paper-
towel-lined plate.

Per Serving: Calories: 426 • Protein: 38 g.
• Carbohydrate: 16 g. • Fat: 22 g.
• Cholesterol: 99 mg. • Sodium: 582 mg.
Exchanges: 1 starch, 4½ lean meat, 2 fat

Panfish Parmesan

Chris Brown – Omaha, Nebraska

½   cup milk
1   egg, beaten
1   cup buttery cracker crumbs
½   cup grated Parmesan cheese
2¼ lbs. sunfish, or substitute,
     fillets (2 to 3 oz. each),
     skin removed
     Vegetable oil

6 servings

In medium mixing bowl, combine milk and egg. In shallow dish, combine
crumbs and Parmesan cheese. Dip fillets first in milk mixture and then
dredge in crumb mixture to coat.

In 12-inch skillet, heat ½ inch oil over medium heat. Add fillets. Fry for
4½ to 6 minutes, or until golden brown, turning over once. Drain on paper-
towel-lined plate.

Per Serving: Calories: 479 • Protein: 37 g. • Carbohydrate: 10 g. • Fat: 32 g.
• Cholesterol: 122 mg. • Sodium: 390 mg.
Exchanges: ⅔ starch, 5 lean meat, 3½ fat

Chinese Fried Fish with Sweet & Sour Sauce

Melvin and Chao Mei Jung – Okemos, Michigan

2¼ lbs. northern pike, or substitute, fillets (6 oz. each), skin removed

MARINADE:
- ¼ cup white wine
- 2 green onions, thinly sliced
- 2 teaspoons soy sauce
- 4 slices peeled fresh gingerroot
- ¼ cup snipped dried black or shiitake mushrooms
- ½ cup hot water

SAUCE:
- ½ cup cold water
- ⅓ cup sugar
- ¼ cup plus 1 tablespoon apple cider vinegar
- 3 tablespoons catsup
- 1 tablespoon sesame oil
- 1½ teaspoons cornstarch
- 1 teaspoon salt

- 1 cup cornstarch
  Vegetable oil

- 2 tablespoons vegetable oil
- ⅓ cup diagonally sliced green onions (1½-inch lengths)
- ⅓ cup grated fresh gingerroot
- 2 to 3 hot chili peppers, seeded and chopped

6 servings

Per Serving: Calories: 403 • Protein: 33 g. • Carbohydrate: 37 g. • Fat: 13 g. • Cholesterol: 66 mg. • Sodium: 585 mg. Exchanges: 1½ starch, 4 lean meat, 1 vegetable, ¾ fruit

How to Prepare Chinese Fried Fish with Sweet & Sour Sauce

ARRANGE fillets in single layer in 13 × 9-inch baking dish. In 1-cup measure, combine marinade ingredients. Pour marinade over fillets, turning to coat. Cover with plastic wrap. Chill at least 30 minutes, turning fillets over once or twice.

PLACE mushrooms in small mixing bowl. Pour hot water over mushrooms. Let soak for 30 minutes, or until softened. Drain and discard liquid. Set mushrooms aside.

COMBINE sauce ingredients in 2-cup measure. Set aside. Place 1 cup cornstarch in shallow dish. Dredge fillets in cornstarch to coat.

Bass Marsala →

David L. Rehrig – Bethlehem, Pennsylvania

⅓ cup all-purpose flour
¼ teaspoon salt
2 tablespoons olive oil
1 tablespoon margarine or butter
1½ lbs. bass, or substitute, fillets
      (6 oz. each), skin removed,
      cut in half crosswise
⅔ cup Marsala wine
⅓ cup snipped fresh parsley
⅛ teaspoon dried oregano leaves

4 servings

In shallow dish, combine flour and salt. Dredge fillets in flour mixture to coat. In 12-inch skillet, heat oil and margarine over medium heat until margarine is melted. Add fillets. Fry for 4 to 8 minutes, or until golden brown, turning over once.

Add Marsala, parsley and oregano to fish in skillet. Cook for 2 to 4 minutes, or until sauce is reduced by half, spooning sauce over fish frequently during cooking. Serve fish with sauce.

Per Serving: Calories: 380 • Protein: 33 g.
• Carbohydrate: 13 g. • Fat: 16 g.
• Cholesterol: 116 mg. • Sodium: 293 mg.
Exchanges: ½ starch, 4½ lean meat,
⅓ fruit, 1½ fat

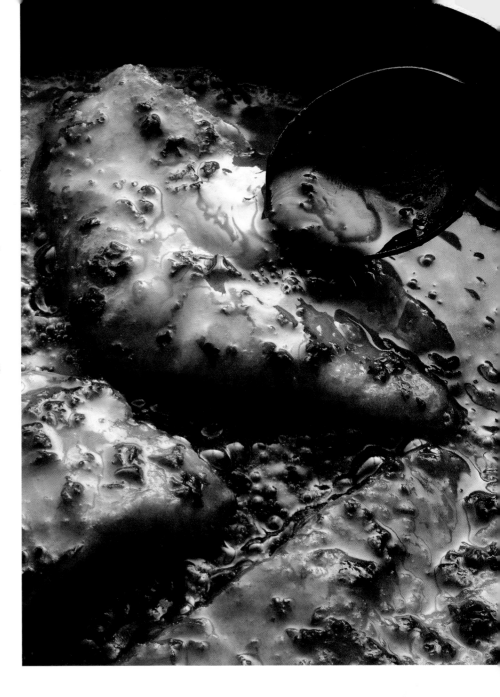

HEAT ½ inch vegetable oil in 12-inch skillet, over medium heat. Add fillets. Fry for 6 to 8 minutes, or until fillets are golden brown, turning over once. Remove fillets from skillet. Place on serving platter. Cover to keep warm. Set aside.

DRAIN and discard oil from skillet. Wipe skillet with paper towels. In same skillet, heat 2 tablespoons vegetable oil over medium heat. Add mushrooms, onions, gingerroot and peppers. Cook for 1 minute.

STIR in sauce mixture. Cook over medium heat for 1½ to 2½ minutes, or until mixture is thickened and translucent, stirring frequently. Spoon sweet and sour sauce over fish.

19

Country Panfried Catfish

Thomas K. Squier – Aberdeen, North Carolina

¼ cup margarine or butter, melted
½ cup all-purpose flour
½ cup white cornmeal
1 tablespoon dried rosemary leaves, crushed
½ teaspoon salt
¼ to ½ teaspoon cayenne
1½ lbs. catfish fillets (6 oz. each), skin removed
   Vegetable oil

4 servings

Place margarine in small mixing bowl. In shallow dish, combine flour, cornmeal, rosemary, salt and cayenne. Dip fillets first in margarine and then dredge in flour mixture to coat.

In 12-inch skillet, heat ⅛ inch oil over medium heat. Add fillets. Fry for 6 to 9 minutes, or until golden brown, turning over once. Drain on paper-towel-lined plate.

Per Serving: Calories: 543 • Protein: 34 g. • Carbohydrate: 26 g. • Fat: 33 g. • Cholesterol: 99 mg. • Sodium: 515 mg. Exchanges: 1¾ starch, 4 lean meat, 4 fat

Pretzel Fish ↑

"This recipe is very simple and works well with any firm-fleshed fish. At one time I was giving the recipe to area restaurants where I live. Whenever we go to friends' houses for fish fries, I am asked to use my recipe."
   Darrell C. Thoma – Omro, Wisconsin

4 cups pretzel twists
2 eggs, beaten
1 can (5 oz.) evaporated milk
3 tablespoons beer or club soda
2¼ lbs. sunfish, northern pike, or substitute, fillets (3 to 6 oz. each), skin removed
   Vegetable oil
   Lemon wedges

6 servings

Place pretzels in food processor. Process until powdery. (Pretzels may also be placed in large plastic food-storage bag and crushed with rolling pin.) Place powdered pretzels in large plastic food-storage bag. In medium mixing bowl, combine eggs, milk and beer. Dip fillets in egg mixture, then shake in pretzel powder to coat.

In 12-inch skillet, heat ⅛ inch oil over medium heat. Add fillets. Fry for 3½ to 6 minutes, or until golden brown, turning over once. Drain on paper-towel-lined plate. Serve with lemon wedges.

Per Serving: Calories: 523 • Protein: 41 g. • Carbohydrate: 32 g. • Fat: 25 g. • Cholesterol: 193 mg. • Sodium: 820 mg. Exchanges: 2 starch, 4¾ lean meat, ¼ skim milk, 2 fat

Gourmet Fried Bass ↑

Thomas K. Squier – Aberdeen, North Carolina

3/4 lb. bass, or substitute, fillets (6 oz. each),
    skin removed, cut in half crosswise
1/4 teaspoon salt
1/8 teaspoon pepper
1/4 cup all-purpose flour
  3 tablespoons margarine or butter, divided
1/2 cup thinly sliced fresh mushrooms
1/4 cup chopped shallots
  1 tablespoon sherry or vermouth
  2 teaspoons fresh lemon juice

2 servings

Sprinkle fillets with salt and pepper. Place flour in
shallow dish. Dredge fillets in flour to coat. In
10-inch skillet, melt 2 tablespoons margarine over
medium heat. Add fillets. Fry for 5 to 7 minutes, or
until golden brown, turning over once. Remove fillets from skillet. Place on serving platter. Cover to
keep warm. Set aside.

Reduce heat to low. In same skillet, melt remaining
1 tablespoon margarine. Add mushrooms and shallots.
Cook for 2 to 3 minutes, or until tender. Stir in sherry
and juice. Spoon mixture over fish.

Per Serving: Calories: 436 • Protein: 35 g. • Carbohydrate: 18 g.
• Fat: 24 g. • Cholesterol: 116 mg. • Sodium: 594 mg.
Exchanges: 3/4 starch, 4 1/2 lean meat, 1 vegetable, 2 fat

Judy B.'s Fried Fish

Judy Belski – Spring Valley, Illinois

COATING:
1/2 cup yellow cornmeal
1/4 cup masa harina (corn flour)
  1 tablespoon baking powder
1 1/2 teaspoons dried parsley flakes, crushed
1/2 teaspoon garlic powder
1/2 teaspoon onion powder
1/2 teaspoon paprika
1/2 teaspoon celery seed
1/4 teaspoon pepper

2 1/4 lbs. any freshwater fish fillets (6 oz. each), skin
    removed
    Vegetable oil

6 servings

In shallow dish, combine coating ingredients.
Dredge fillets in coating to coat. In 12-inch skillet,
heat 1/8 inch oil over medium heat. Add fillets. Fry
for 5 to 7 minutes, or until golden brown, turning
over once. Drain on paper-towel-lined plate. Top
with salsa, if desired.

Per Serving: Calories: 419 • Protein: 34 g. • Carbohydrate: 13 g.
• Fat: 25 g. • Cholesterol: 116 mg. • Sodium: 334 mg.
Exchanges: 1 starch, 4 1/2 lean meat, 2 1/4 fat

← Pan-roasted Northern Pike

Tim Anderson – Minneapolis, Minnesota

1½ lbs. northern pike, or substitute, fillets
    (6 oz. each), skin removed
½ teaspoon salt
¼ cup all-purpose flour
¼ cup vegetable oil
¼ cup diagonally sliced green onions
    (½-inch lengths)
1 oz. fully cooked ham, cut into 2 × ¼-inch strips
    (about ¼ cup)
¼ cup orange juice
3 tablespoons ready-to-serve chicken broth
½ cup margarine or butter, divided
½ cup snipped fresh chives or parsley

4 servings

Sprinkle fillets with salt. Place flour in shallow dish. Dredge fillets in flour to coat.

In 12-inch skillet, heat oil over medium heat. Add fillets. Fry for 5 to 7 minutes, or until golden brown, turning over once. Add onions and ham. Toss to coat. Add juice and broth. Reduce heat to low. Cover. Cook for 2 to 3 minutes, or until fish is firm and opaque and just begins to flake. Transfer fillets to serving platter. Cover to keep warm. Set aside.

Bring mixture in skillet to a simmer over medium heat. Cook for 2 to 3 minutes, or until reduced to about ¼ cup. Add ¼ cup margarine. Stir until melted. Add remaining ¼ cup margarine. Stir until melted. Stir in chives. Spoon sauce over fish.

Per Serving: Calories: 530 • Protein: 36 g. • Carbohydrate: 9 g.
• Fat: 39 g. • Cholesterol: 72 mg. • Sodium: 790 mg.
Exchanges: ½ starch, 4¾ lean meat, ⅓ fruit, 4¾ fat

Sam's Cajun Fried Fish

Sam Sola – Grandview, Missouri

½ cup buttermilk baking mix
¼ cup milk
1 egg white
1 cup yellow cornmeal
½ teaspoon cayenne
½ teaspoon garlic powder
½ teaspoon black pepper
½ teaspoon white pepper
½ teaspoon salt (optional)
1½ lbs. any freshwater fish fillets (6 oz. each), skin
    removed
    Vegetable oil

4 servings

In medium mixing bowl, beat together baking mix, milk and egg white. In shallow dish, combine remaining ingredients, except fish and oil. Dip fillets first in batter and then dredge in cornmeal mixture to coat.

In 12-inch skillet, heat ⅛ inch oil over medium heat. Add fillets. Fry for 6 to 8½ minutes, or until golden brown, turning over once. Drain on paper-towel-lined plate.

Per Serving: Calories: 575 • Protein: 38 g. • Carbohydrate: 38 g.
• Fat: 30 g. • Cholesterol: 118 mg. • Sodium: 316 mg.
Exchanges: 2½ starch, 4 lean meat, 3½ fat

Pecan-coated Fried Fish

Wayne Phillips – Saskatoon, Saskatchewan

  2   eggs, beaten
 ¼   teaspoon salt
 ¼   teaspoon pepper
 ¾   cup unseasoned dry bread crumbs
 ¾   cup ground pecans
2¼ lbs. any freshwater fish fillets (6 oz. each), skin
      removed
      Vegetable oil
 ⅓   cup margarine or butter
  1   tablespoon fresh lemon juice
 ⅛   to ¼ teaspoon cayenne

6 servings

In medium mixing bowl, combine eggs, salt and pepper. In shallow dish, combine bread crumbs and pecans. Dip fillets first in egg mixture and then dredge in bread crumb mixture to coat.

In 12-inch skillet, heat ⅛ inch oil over medium heat. Add fillets. Fry for 5 to 8 minutes, or until golden brown, turning over once. Wipe out skillet with paper towels. In same skillet, melt margarine over medium heat. Stir in juice and cayenne. Spoon sauce over fish.

Per Serving: Calories: 515 • Protein: 37 g. • Carbohydrate: 12 g. • Fat: 35 g. • Cholesterol: 138 mg. • Sodium: 387 mg.
Exchanges: ¾ starch, 5 lean meat, 4 fat

Honey-fried Walleye Fillets ↑

"This recipe has been handed down through the years in our family."
Elaine H. Drew – Delano, Minnesota

  1   egg, beaten
  1   teaspoon honey
  1   cup coarsely crushed soda crackers
 ⅓   cup all-purpose flour
 ¼   teaspoon salt
 ¼   teaspoon pepper
1½ lbs. walleye, or substitute, fillets (6 oz. each),
      skin removed
      Vegetable oil

4 servings

In small mixing bowl, combine egg and honey. In shallow dish, combine crackers, flour, salt and pepper. Dip fillets first in egg mixture and then dredge in cracker mixture to coat.

In 12-inch skillet, heat ⅛ inch oil over medium heat. Add fillets. Fry for 4 to 7 minutes, or until golden brown, turning over once. Drain on paper-towel-lined plate. Serve with lemon wedges and additional honey for drizzling, if desired.

Per Serving: Calories: 417 • Protein: 37 g. • Carbohydrate: 22 g. • Fat: 19 g. • Cholesterol: 120 mg. • Sodium: 430 mg.
Exchanges: 1½ starch, 4¾ lean meat, 1 fat

Bass Picasso

Albia Dugger – Miami, Florida

2¼ lbs. bass, or substitute, fillets
      (6 oz. each), skin removed,
      cut in half crosswise
3 tablespoons lemon juice,
      divided
1 tablespoon Worcestershire sauce
2 tablespoons olive oil
4 slices peeled fresh gingerroot
½ cup all-purpose flour
2 eggs, beaten
1 teaspoon plus dash red pepper
      sauce, divided
¼ teaspoon salt
¼ cup plus 2 tablespoons
      margarine or butter
1 medium green apple, cored,
      quartered and thinly sliced
1 medium tomato, seeded and
      chopped (1 cup)
2 medium bananas, sliced
1 jar (2 oz.) diced pimiento,
      drained
¼ cup red currant jelly

6 servings

Arrange fillets in single layer in 13 × 9-inch baking dish. Sprinkle evenly with 1 tablespoon juice and the Worcestershire sauce. Cover with plastic wrap. Chill at least 15 minutes. Heat oven to 350°F. Place large ovenproof serving platter in oven.

In 12-inch skillet, heat oil over medium heat. Add gingerroot. Cook for 1 minute, or until tender. Remove skillet from heat. Chop gingerroot. Set aside.

Place flour in shallow dish. In small mixing bowl, combine eggs and 1 teaspoon red pepper sauce. Pat fillets dry with paper towels. Sprinkle with salt.

In same skillet, melt 2 tablespoons margarine over medium heat. Dredge fillets first in flour and then dip in egg mixture. Increase heat to medium-high. Add fillets. Fry for 4 to 6 minutes, or just until brown, turning over once. Remove fillets from skillet. Place in oven on serving platter. Bake for 7 to 10 minutes, or until fish is firm and opaque and just begins to flake.

Meanwhile, in 12-inch skillet, melt remaining ¼ cup margarine over medium heat. Add gingerroot, apple, tomato, bananas and pimiento. Cook for 1½ to 2 minutes, or until mixture is warm, stirring gently several times during cooking. Add jelly, the remaining 2 tablespoons juice and dash of red pepper sauce. Cook for 1½ to 2 minutes, or until jelly is melted. Spoon sauce over fish.

Per Serving: Calories: 495 • Protein: 36 g. • Carbohydrate: 33 g. • Fat: 24 g. • Cholesterol: 187 mg. • Sodium: 420 mg.
Exchanges: ½ starch, 5 lean meat, 1⅔ fruit, 1¾ fat

Caraway Rye →
Coated Fried Fish

Wayne Phillips –
Saskatoon, Saskatchewan

  2 eggs, beaten
¼ teaspoon salt
¼ teaspoon pepper
  6 slices caraway rye bread,
      trimmed, dried and crumbled
      (¾ cup)
  1 tablespoon plus 1½ teaspoons
      dried oregano leaves
2¼ lbs. any freshwater fish fillets
      (6 oz. each), skin removed
      Vegetable oil

TOMATO SAUCE:
  ½ cup tomato sauce
  2 tablespoons white wine or
      half-and-half
  ½ teaspoon sugar

6 servings

In medium mixing bowl, combine eggs, salt and pepper. In shallow dish, combine bread crumbs and oregano. Dip fillets first in egg mixture and then dredge in crumb mixture to coat.

In 12-inch skillet, heat ⅛ inch oil over medium heat. Add fillets. Fry for 5 to 8 minutes, or until golden brown, turning over once. Drain on paper-towel-lined plate.

In 8-inch skillet, combine sauce ingredients. Simmer over medium-low heat for 5 to 7 minutes, or until sauce is hot and slightly reduced. Spoon sauce over fish.

Per Serving: Calories: 410 • Protein: 38 g.
• Carbohydrate: 16 g. • Fat: 21 g.
• Cholesterol: 137 mg. • Sodium: 440 mg.
Exchanges: 1 starch, 4¾ lean meat,
¼ vegetable, 1¼ fat

Panfried Panfish

"This is the recipe my mother-in-law used when cooking a Good Friday fish dinner. I added the Cajun seasoning for a little more spice."
   Glen Laurion – Orland, Indiana

⅓ cup seasoned coating mix
¼ teaspoon paprika
¼ teaspoon pepper
¼ teaspoon Cajun seasoning
    (optional)

¾ cup seasoned bread crumbs
  2 eggs, beaten
  1 lb. sunfish, or substitute, fillets
      (2 to 3 oz. each), skin removed
¼ cup plus 2 tablespoons margarine
    or butter

2 to 3 servings

In large plastic food-storage bag, combine coating mix, paprika, pepper and Cajun seasoning. In another large plastic food-storage bag, place bread crumbs. Place eggs in medium mixing bowl. Shake fillets first in coating mixture, then dip in eggs, then shake in bread crumbs to coat.

In 10-inch skillet, melt margarine over medium heat. Add fillets. Fry for 4 to 5½ minutes, or until golden brown, turning over once. Drain on paper-towel-lined plate.

Per Serving: Calories: 557 • Protein: 40 g. • Carbohydrate: 30 g. • Fat: 30 g.
• Cholesterol: 245 mg. • Sodium: 1778 mg.
Exchanges: 2 starch, 4¾ lean meat, 3 fat

Oat Bran Coated Fried Fish

Wayne Phillips – Saskatoon, Saskatchewan

- 2 eggs, beaten
- 1/4 teaspoon salt
- 1/4 teaspoon pepper
- 1 cup oat bran
- 2 1/4 lbs. any freshwater fish fillets (6 oz. each), skin removed
  Vegetable oil

LIME DILL SAUCE:
- 1/2 cup mayonnaise
- 1 tablespoon plus 1 1/2 teaspoons fresh lime juice
- 2 tablespoons plus 1 1/2 teaspoons snipped fresh dill weed

6 servings

In medium mixing bowl, combine eggs, salt and pepper. Place oat bran in shallow dish. Dip fillets first in egg mixture and then dredge in oat bran to coat.

In 12-inch skillet, heat 1/8 inch oil over medium heat. Add fillets. Fry for 5 to 8 minutes, or until golden brown, turning over once.

In small mixing bowl, combine sauce ingredients. Spoon sauce over fish.

Per Serving: Calories: 511 • Protein: 37 g. • Carbohydrate: 12 g. • Fat: 37 g. • Cholesterol: 197 mg. • Sodium: 336 mg.
Exchanges: 3/4 starch, 5 lean meat, 4 1/3 fat

South Louisiana Fish Fry ↑

"Place leftovers in the refrigerator, cover with paper towels and eat cold the next day; it's even better!"
Ken Beck – Baton Rouge, Louisiana

- 1 large green or red pepper, thinly sliced into rings
- 1 medium onion, cut in half lengthwise, then thinly sliced crosswise
- 1 cup seasoned coating mix
- 2 1/4 lbs. catfish, bass, or substitute, fillets (6 oz. each), skin removed, cut into 1 1/2-inch pieces
  Vegetable oil

6 servings

Heat oven to 175°F. Place half of pepper and onion slices into large paper grocery bag. Set aside. Place cornmeal mix in large plastic food-storage bag. Add fish, a few pieces at a time. Shake to coat.

In 10-inch skillet, heat 1/2 inch oil over medium heat. Add half of fish. Fry for 3 1/2 to 5 minutes, or until golden brown, turning over occasionally. With slotted spoon, remove fish from skillet. Place immediately into grocery bag. Hold bag closed. Shake gently. Add remaining pepper and onion slices to bag. Close bag. Repeat with remaining fish. Remove fish and vegetables from grocery bag and place in paper-towel-lined baking dish. Place in warm oven until ready to serve.

Per Serving: Calories: 405 • Protein: 34 g. • Carbohydrate: 16 g. • Fat: 22 g. • Cholesterol: 99 mg. • Sodium: 945 mg.
Exchanges: 1 starch, 4 1/4 lean meat, 1/2 vegetable, 1 3/4 fat

Italian-flavored Bass ↑

Don Will – Poughkeepsie, New York

¾ lb. bass, or substitute, fillets (6 oz. each), skin removed, cut into 1½ to 2-inch pieces
½ cup milk
1 egg, beaten
1 tablespoon water
1 cup seasoned dry bread crumbs
2 tablespoons margarine or butter
2 tablespoons peanut oil

2 servings

Place fish in small mixing bowl. Pour milk over fish. Stir to coat. Cover with plastic wrap. Chill 30 minutes. In another small mixing bowl, combine egg and water. Drain and discard milk from fish. Place fish in egg mixture. Stir to coat. Cover with plastic wrap. Chill 15 minutes.

Drain and discard egg mixture from fish. Place bread crumbs in shallow dish. Dredge fish in crumbs to coat.

In 10-inch skillet, heat margarine and oil over medium heat. Add fish. Fry for 3 to 4 minutes, or until golden brown, turning over once. Drain on paper-towel-lined plate.

Per Serving: Calories: 666 • Protein: 43 g. • Carbohydrate: 42 g. • Fat: 35 g. • Cholesterol: 176 mg. • Sodium: 1873 mg. Exchanges: 2½ starch, 5 lean meat, 4 fat

Mustard Batter Fish

Michael B. Reilly – Lafayette, Louisiana

⅓ cup prepared or Dijon mustard
¼ cup plus 1 tablespoon water
1 teaspoon fresh lemon juice
1 teaspoon Worcestershire sauce
⅛ teaspoon cayenne
1½ cups seasoned coating mix
2¼ lbs. any freshwater fish fillets (6 oz. each), skin removed, cut into 1½-inch pieces
Vegetable oil

6 servings

In small mixing bowl, combine mustard, water, juice, Worcestershire sauce and cayenne. Place coating mix in shallow dish. Dip fish first in mustard mixture and then dredge in coating mix to coat.

In 10-inch skillet, heat ½ inch oil over medium heat. Add fish. Fry for 3 to 4 minutes, or until golden brown, turning over once. Drain on paper-towel-lined plate.

Per Serving: Calories: 504 • Protein: 37 g. • Carbohydrate: 21 g. • Fat: 30 g. • Cholesterol: 116 mg. • Sodium: 1556 mg. Exchanges: 1½ starch, 4½ lean meat, 3¼ fat

Panfried Trout Leeper Keeper

Merton D. Leeper – Littleton, Colorado

1½ lbs. stream trout, or substitute, fillets (2 oz. each), skin removed, cut into 2-inch pieces
1½ cups beer or white wine

COATING:
  1 cup yellow cornmeal
  1 teaspoon chili powder
  ½ teaspoon onion powder
  ½ teaspoon celery salt
  ¼ teaspoon garlic powder
  ¼ teaspoon paprika
  ¼ teaspoon pepper
  ⅛ teaspoon cayenne

     Vegetable oil

4 servings

Arrange fish pieces, slightly overlapping, in 11 × 7-inch baking dish. Pour beer over fish. Cover with plastic wrap. Chill at least 30 minutes. Drain and discard beer from fish.

In large plastic food-storage bag, combine coating ingredients. Add fish, a few pieces at a time. Shake to coat. In 10-inch skillet, heat ½ inch oil over medium heat. Add fish. Fry for 3 to 4 minutes, or until golden brown, turning over once. Drain on paper-towel-lined plate.

Per Serving: Calories: 398 • Protein: 38 g. • Carbohydrate: 28 g. • Fat: 13 g. • Cholesterol: 97 mg. • Sodium: 233 mg.
Exchanges: 1¾ starch, 4½ lean meat

Fish Cakes ↑

Thomas K. Squier – Aberdeen, North Carolina

  2 cups any flaked cooked freshwater fish
  1 cup cornflake crumbs
  ½ cup sliced green onions
  3 eggs, divided
  1 tablespoon sherry
  1 tablespoon Worcestershire sauce
  1 teaspoon sesame oil (optional)
  ¼ teaspoon salt
  ¼ teaspoon pepper
  ½ cup seasoned dry bread crumbs
  2 tablespoons vegetable oil

3 servings

In medium mixing bowl, combine fish, cornflake crumbs, onions, 1 egg, the sherry, Worcestershire sauce, sesame oil, salt and pepper. Divide mixture into 6 equal portions. Shape each portion into ½-inch-thick patties.

In small mixing bowl, lightly beat remaining 2 eggs. Place bread crumbs in shallow dish. Dip patties first in eggs and then dredge in crumbs to coat.

In 10-inch skillet, heat vegetable oil over medium heat. Add patties. Fry for 2 to 4 minutes, or until golden brown, turning over once. Drain on paper-towel-lined plate. Serve with lemon wedges, tartar sauce or cocktail sauce, if desired.

Per Serving: Calories: 543 • Protein: 40 g. • Carbohydrate: 50 g. • Fat: 19 g. • Cholesterol: 289 mg. • Sodium: 1333 mg.
Exchanges: 3⅓ starch, 4 lean meat, 1½ fat

Missouri Levee Frog Legs

Ken and Donna White –
Independence, Missouri

2 lbs. frog legs (about 6 pairs),
     skin removed
   Salt
   Pepper
½ cup margarine or butter
½ cup chopped shallots
½ cup sliced fresh mushrooms
½ cup white wine
2 tablespoons fresh lemon juice
2 tablespoons snipped fresh
     parsley

2 to 3 servings

Sprinkle frog legs lightly with salt
and pepper. In 12-inch skillet, melt
margarine over medium heat. Add
legs to skillet, turning to coat. Fry
for 8 to 10 minutes, or until browned
on both sides, turning over once.

Add shallots and mushrooms. Reduce heat to medium-low. Simmer
for 5 minutes. Add wine and juice.
Simmer for 5 to 6 minutes, or until
legs are tender and meat near bone
is no longer pink.

Arrange legs on serving platter.
Spoon shallot and mushroom
mixture over legs. Before serving,
sprinkle evenly with parsley.

Per Serving: Calories: 467 • Protein: 34 g.
• Carbohydrate: 7 g. • Fat: 31 g
• Cholesterol: 98 mg. • Sodium: 477 mg.
Exchanges: 4½ lean meat, ½ vegetable,
⅓ fruit, 3½ fat

Deep-fried Corona® Catfish ↑

"A special, spicy batter for a superb catfish feast. Also makes an excellent batter for deep-frying shrimp."
Duffy Soto – Lake City, Florida

1   cup all-purpose flour, sifted
1   cup Corona® beer, divided
⅓   cup finely chopped onion
1   tablespoon olive or vegetable oil
1½ teaspoons salt-free herb and
       spice blend
1½ teaspoons Cajun seasoning
⅛   teaspoon red pepper sauce
     Vegetable oil
2¼ lbs. catfish fillets (6 oz. each),
       skin removed, cut in half
       crosswise

6 servings

In medium mixing bowl, combine flour, ¾ cup beer, the onion, olive oil,
spice blend and Cajun seasonings. Stir in remaining ¼ cup beer and the
pepper sauce. Cover with plastic wrap. Set aside at room temperature for
30 minutes.

In deep-fat fryer, heat 2 inches vegetable oil to 375°F. Dip fish in batter to
coat. In hot oil, fry fish, a few pieces at a time, for 5 to 6 minutes, or until
golden brown, turning over once. Drain on paper-towel-lined plate.

Per Serving: Calories: 389 • Protein: 33 g. • Carbohydrate: 19 g. • Fat: 18 g.
• Cholesterol: 99 mg. • Sodium: 324 mg.
Exchanges: 1¼ starch, 4¼ lean meat, 1 fat

←Fritos® Fillets

Robert L. Hirt II – Reelsville, Indiana

2¼ lbs. any freshwater fish fillets
　　(6 oz. each), skin removed,
　　cut in half crosswise
3 cups beer, divided
1 tablespoon fresh lemon juice
　　Vegetable oil
2 eggs, beaten
1 tablespoon olive oil
2 cups finely crushed Fritos®
　　corn chips
2 tablespoons grated Parmesan
　　cheese
1 teaspoon cayenne

6 servings

Arrange fillets, slightly overlapping, in 13 × 9-inch baking dish. Pour 2¼ cups beer and the juice over fillets. Cover with plastic wrap. Chill 1 hour.

In deep-fat fryer, heat 2 inches vegetable oil to 375°F. Drain and discard beer mixture from fish. Pat fillets dry with paper towels.

In medium mixing bowl, combine remaining ¾ cup beer, the eggs and olive oil. In shallow dish, combine remaining ingredients. Dip fish first in beer mixture and then dredge in Fritos® mixture to coat. In hot oil, fry fish, a few pieces at a time, for 3 to 4 minutes, or until golden brown, turning over once. Drain on paper-towel-lined plate.

Per Serving: Calories: 491 • Protein: 37 g.
• Carbohydrate: 18 g. • Fat: 28 g.
• Cholesterol: 188 mg. • Sodium: 387 mg.
Exchanges: 1¼ starch, 4½ lean meat, 3 fat

Buttermilk Bass

Randall J. Hudson – Cairo, Georgia

　　Vegetable oil
1 cup buttermilk
2 cups yellow cornmeal
2 teaspoons garlic salt
2 teaspoons seasoned salt or salt
1 teaspoon pepper
2¼ lbs. bass, or substitute, fillets
　　(6 oz. each), skin removed,
　　cut in half crosswise

6 servings

In deep-fat fryer, heat 2 inches oil to 375°F. Place buttermilk in shallow dish. In second shallow dish, combine cornmeal, garlic salt, seasoned salt and pepper. Dip fillets first in buttermilk and then dredge in cornmeal mixture to coat. In hot oil, fry fillets, a few at a time, for 3 to 4 minutes, or until golden brown, turning over once. Drain on paper-towel-lined plate.

Per Serving: Calories: 522 • Protein: 37 g. • Carbohydrate: 39 g. • Fat: 23 g.
• Cholesterol: 117 mg. • Sodium: 1185 mg.
Exchanges: 2¼ starch, 4 lean meat, ¼ skim milk, 2 fat

Paulie's Pie-eyed Fish

"This dish is very good served with sliced onions, mushrooms and green peppers that have been simmered in Worcestershire sauce and spooned over rice."

Paul R. Gosselin – Schaghticoke, New York

  2 cans (12 oz. each) beer
  2 eggs, beaten
  3 bay leaves
  ½ teaspoon dried thyme leaves
  ½ teaspoon dried marjoram leaves
  ¼ teaspoon salt
  ¼ teaspoon freshly ground pepper
2¼ lbs. any freshwater fish fillets
      (6 oz. each), skin removed,
      cut in half crosswise

Sauce:
  1 cup spaghetti sauce
  1 tablespoon fresh lemon juice
  2 teaspoons prepared horseradish
  ¼ teaspoon red pepper sauce
      Vegetable oil
  1 cup unseasoned dry bread
      crumbs
      Lemon wedges

6 servings

Per Serving: Calories: 410 • Protein: 36 g.
• Carbohydrate: 20 g. • Fat: 20 g.
• Cholesterol: 134 mg. • Sodium: 593 mg.
Exchanges: 1 starch, 4¼ lean meat,
1 vegetable, 1¼ fat

How to Prepare Paulie's Pie-eyed Fish

COMBINE beer, eggs, bay leaves, thyme, marjoram, salt and pepper in large mixing bowl. Add fish. Cover with plastic wrap. Refrigerate overnight.

COMBINE sauce ingredients in small mixing bowl. Cover with plastic wrap. Chill at least 1 hour.

HEAT 2 inches oil to 375°F in deep-fat fryer. Drain and discard beer mixture and bay leaves from fillets. Place crumbs in shallow dish. Dredge fillets in crumbs to coat.

FRY fish in hot oil, a few pieces at a time, for 3 to 4 minutes, or until golden brown, turning over once. Drain on paper-towel-lined plate. Serve with sauce and lemon wedges.

Buttermilk Delight ↑

"Especially good with bass, walleye, perch and all panfish."
  Elton L. Martelli – Canton, Ohio

2½ cups buttermilk
2¼ lbs. any freshwater fish fillets (6 oz. each), skin
     removed, cut in half crosswise
     Vegetable oil
 ¾ cup self-rising flour*
 ¾ cup yellow cornmeal
1½ teaspoons onion salt

6 servings

Place buttermilk in medium mixing bowl. Add
fish. Stir to coat. Cover with plastic wrap. Chill
45 minutes.

In deep-fat fryer, heat 2 inches oil to 375°F. In shal-
low dish, combine flour, cornmeal and onion salt.
Drain and discard buttermilk from fish pieces.
Dredge fish in flour mixture to coat.

In hot oil, fry fish, a few pieces at a time, for 3 to 4
minutes, or until golden brown, turning over once.
Drain on paper-towel-lined plate. Serve with tartar
sauce, cocktail sauce, sweet and sour sauce or salsa,
if desired.

*You may substitute all-purpose flour for self-rising
flour by adding 1½ teaspoons baking powder and
½ teaspoon salt.

Per Serving: Calories: 447 • Protein: 36 g. • Carbohydrate: 27 g.
• Fat: 21 g. • Cholesterol: 117 mg. • Sodium: 758 mg.
Exchanges: 1¾ starch, 4½ lean meat, 1½ fat

Gingered Beer-battered Bass

"Kids love them! They call them Bass McNuggets."
  Barbara Reid Alcamo – Spring, Texas

     Vegetable oil
 1 cup cornstarch
 2 eggs, separated
 ¾ cup beer
 2 tablespoons soy sauce
 ½ teaspoon ground ginger
 ½ teaspoon dry mustard
 ½ teaspoon salt, divided
 1 cup all-purpose flour
 ¼ teaspoon pepper
1½ lbs. bass, or substitute, fillets (6 oz. each), skin
     removed, cut into 1½-inch pieces

4 servings

In deep-fat fryer, heat 2 inches oil to 375°F. In medium mixing bowl, combine cornstarch, egg yolks,
beer, soy sauce, ginger, mustard and ¼ teaspoon salt.
Set aside.

In another medium mixing bowl, beat egg whites
at high speed of electric mixer until stiff but not
dry. Fold into beer batter.

In shallow dish, combine flour, remaining ¼ teaspoon salt and the pepper. Dip fish first in batter and
then dredge in flour mixture to coat. In hot oil, fry
fish, a few pieces at a time, for 3 to 4 minutes, or
until golden brown, turning over once. Drain on
paper-towel-lined plate.

Per Serving: Calories: 560 • Protein: 39 g. • Carbohydrate: 56 g.
• Fat: 17 g. • Cholesterol: 222 mg. • Sodium: 944 mg.
Exchanges: 3½ starch, 4¼ lean meat, 1 fat

Crappie Fritters →

Al Weber – Glendale, New York

½ cup white wine
½ cup water
1 lb. crappie, or substitute, fillets
　 (2 to 3 oz. each), skin removed
　 Vegetable oil
¼ cup thinly sliced green onions
¼ cup unseasoned dry bread
　 crumbs
2 eggs, beaten
2 tablespoons finely chopped
　 onion
2 tablespoons tartar sauce
1 tablespoon snipped fresh parsley
½ teaspoon salt
¼ teaspoon pepper
7 to 10 drops red pepper sauce
1 cup crushed soda crackers

3 to 4 servings

In 10-inch skillet, heat wine and water over medium heat until boiling. Add fillets. Cover. Reduce heat to low. Simmer for 5 to 7 minutes, or until fish is firm and opaque and just begins to flake. Drain and discard liquid from fish. Flake fish with fork. Set aside.

In deep-fat fryer, heat 2 inches oil to 375°F. In large mixing bowl, combine remaining ingredients, except cracker crumbs. Add fish. Mix well. Form fish mixture into twenty 1½-inch-diameter balls. Place cracker crumbs in shallow dish. Roll balls in crumbs to coat.

In hot oil, fry balls, 5 or 6 at a time, for 2 to 3 minutes, or until golden brown, turning over once. Drain on paper-towel-lined plate. Serve with tartar sauce, cocktail sauce, sweet and sour sauce or salsa, if desired.

Per Serving: Calories: 383 • Protein: 28 g. • Carbohydrate: 19 g. • Fat: 20 g. • Cholesterol: 186 mg. • Sodium: 693 mg. Exchanges: 1¼ starch, 3½ lean meat, 2 fat

Fish Croquettes

Viola DesRosiers – Thunder Bay, Ontario

　 Vegetable oil
2 cups any flaked cooked
　 freshwater fish
2 cups cooked mashed potatoes
1 cup shredded Cheddar cheese
2 eggs, beaten
3 tablespoons finely chopped
　 onion
2 tablespoons snipped fresh
　 parsley
1 teaspoon lemon pepper
¾ teaspoon garlic powder
½ teaspoon salt-free herb and
　 spice blend
⅓ cup all-purpose flour

3 to 4 servings

In deep-fat fryer, heat 2 inches oil to 375°F. In medium mixing bowl, combine all ingredients, except flour. With floured hands, form fish mixture into twenty-eight 1½-inch-diameter balls. Place flour in shallow dish. Roll balls in flour to coat. In hot oil, fry balls, 5 or 6 at a time, for 2 to 3 minutes, or until golden brown, turning over once. Drain on paper-towel-lined plate. Serve with tartar sauce, cocktail sauce, sweet and sour sauce or salsa, if desired.

Per Serving: Calories: 517 • Protein: 33 g. • Carbohydrate: 28 g. • Fat: 31 g. • Cholesterol: 177 mg. • Sodium: 759 mg. Exchanges: 1¾ starch, 4 lean meat, 3¾ fat

33

Crappie Oriental

Larry Whiteley – Springfield, Missouri

⅓ cup vegetable oil
1 small onion, cut into 12 wedges
1 cup sliced celery
2 cups fresh snow pea pods
½ cup carrot strips (2 × ¼-inch strips)
4 oz. fresh mushrooms, sliced (1 cup)

2 tablespoons sherry
1 tablespoon plus 1½ teaspoons soy sauce
½ teaspoon ground ginger
1 lb. crappie, or substitute, fillets (2 to 3 oz. each), skin removed
1½ teaspoons cornstarch mixed with 1 tablespoon cold water

4 servings

In 12-inch skillet or wok, heat oil over medium-high heat. Add onion and celery. Stir-fry for 1 to 1½ minutes, or until vegetables are tender-crisp. With slotted spoon, remove vegetables from skillet. Cover to keep warm. Set aside.

To same skillet, add pea pods and carrot. Stir-fry for 2 to 3 minutes, or until color brightens. With slotted spoon, remove vegetables from skillet and add to celery mixture. Add mushrooms to skillet. Stir-fry for 1 to 2 minutes, or until tender.

Add sherry, soy sauce and ginger to skillet. Return vegetables to skillet, stirring to combine. Add fillets. Stir gently to combine. Reduce heat to medium. Cover. Simmer for 4 to 5 minutes, or until fish is firm and opaque and just begins to flake.

Stir cornstarch mixture into liquid in skillet. Cook for 1 to 1½ minutes, or until sauce is thickened and translucent, stirring frequently. Serve over hot cooked rice, if desired.

Per Serving: Calories: 329 • Protein: 25 g. • Carbohydrate: 12 g. • Fat: 19 g.
• Cholesterol: 76 mg. • Sodium: 512 mg.
Exchanges: 3 lean meat, 2½ vegetable, 2 fat

←Wok Fish Sun

Chris Langer – Richmond, Minnesota

1½ lbs. sunfish, or substitute, fillets (2 to 3 oz. each), skin removed
1½ teaspoons cornstarch
1 tablespoon water
1 teaspoon sesame oil
½ teaspoon salt
¼ teaspoon white vinegar
⅛ teaspoon five-spice powder
2 tablespoons vegetable oil
2 cloves garlic, minced
4 slices peeled fresh gingerroot
2 medium tomatoes, each cut into 8 wedges
1 pkg. (9 oz.) frozen sugar snap peas, defrosted
1 medium red pepper, cut into 1-inch chunks
1 medium green pepper, cut into 1-inch chunks
½ cup thinly sliced green onions
2 tablespoons soy sauce

4 servings

Arrange fillets, slightly overlapping, in 13 × 9-inch baking dish. In small bowl, combine cornstarch, water, sesame oil, salt, vinegar and five-spice powder. Spread cornstarch mixture evenly over fillets, turning to coat. Cover dish with plastic wrap. Chill 1 hour.

In wok, heat vegetable oil over medium-high heat. Add garlic and gingerroot. Stir-fry for 30 seconds, or until browned, stirring constantly. Using slotted spoon, remove and discard garlic and gingerroot from oil. Add fish. Stir-fry for 3 to 5 minutes, or until fish is firm and opaque and just begins to flake. Remove fish from wok. Place on serving platter. Cover to keep warm. Set aside.

Add remaining ingredients to wok. Stir-fry for 3 to 4 minutes, or until mixture is hot, stirring constantly. Stir in fish. Serve over hot cooked rice, if desired.

Per Serving: Calories: 303 • Protein: 37 g.
• Carbohydrate: 17 g. • Fat: 9 g.
• Cholesterol: 114 mg. • Sodium: 937 mg.
Exchanges: 4 lean meat, 3 vegetable

Chinese-style Fish with Vegetables

"You can substitute almost any vegetables including zucchini, cabbage, celery, broccoli, cauliflower or snow pea pods."
Reiko Andersons – Sylvania, Ohio

½ oz. dried shiitake mushrooms
1½ cups hot water
1½ lbs. walleye, or substitute, fillets (6 oz. each), skin removed, cut into 1-inch pieces
½ teaspoon salt
1 egg white, beaten
3 tablespoons cornstarch

SAUCE:
1 tablespoon plus 1 teaspoon cornstarch
1 tablespoon sugar
1 teaspoon instant chicken bouillon granules
1¼ cups reserved mushroom liquid
2 tablespoons soy sauce
1 tablespoon rice wine vinegar
1 tablespoon dry sherry
½ teaspoon sesame oil

2 tablespoons vegetable oil
1 clove garlic, minced
1 teaspoon grated fresh gingerroot
1 medium green pepper, cut into 1-inch pieces
1 medium red pepper, cut into 1-inch pieces
1 medium carrot, cut into 2 × ¼-inch strips
1 small onion, cut into 12 wedges
½ cup diagonally sliced green onions (1½-inch lengths)

4 servings

Place mushrooms in small mixing bowl. Pour hot water over mushrooms. Let soak for 30 minutes, or until softened. Drain liquid, reserving 1¼ cups. Slice mushrooms. Set aside.

Place fish in medium mixing bowl. Sprinkle with salt. Add egg white. Stir to coat. Sprinkle cornstarch over fish mixture. Toss to coat. Set aside.

In small mixing bowl, combine sauce ingredients. Set aside. In wok, heat ½ cup water over medium-high heat until boiling. Spray round cooking rack with nonstick vegetable cooking spray. Arrange fish on prepared rack. Set rack in wok about 1½ inches above water. Cover. Steam for 3 to 5 minutes, or until fish is firm and opaque and just begins to flake. Remove from heat. Set aside.

Drain and discard water from wok. Wipe out wok with paper towels. In same wok, heat vegetable oil over high heat. Add garlic and gingerroot. Stir in mushrooms and remaining ingredients. Stir-fry for 3 to 4 minutes, or until onion is tender-crisp. Add fish. Stir-fry for 1 to 2 minutes, or until hot, stirring gently. Add sauce mixture. Cook for 1 to 2 minutes, or until sauce is thickened and translucent, stirring constantly. Serve over hot cooked rice, if desired.

Per Serving: Calories: 326 • Protein: 35 g. • Carbohydrate: 22 g. • Fat: 10 g. • Cholesterol: 146 mg. • Sodium: 1141 mg.
Exchanges: ½ starch, 4 lean meat, 3 vegetable

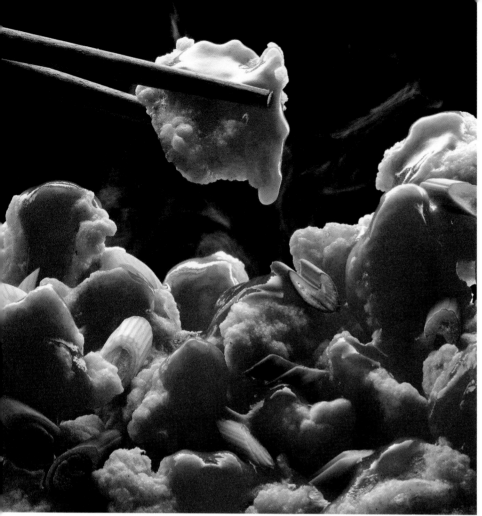

Catfish Marie

Jude W. Theriot – Lake Charles, Louisiana

1 teaspoon grated orange peel	3 tablespoons vegetable oil, divided
½ cup fresh orange juice	2¼ lbs. catfish fillets (6 oz. each), skin removed, cut into ¾-inch pieces
2 tablespoons fresh lemon juice	
2 teaspoons cornstarch	
1 teaspoon salt	2 cups fresh snow pea pods
½ teaspoon red pepper sauce	1½ cups shredded red cabbage
½ teaspoon freshly ground pepper	Orange slices

4 servings

In 1-cup measure, combine peel, juices, cornstarch, salt, red pepper sauce and pepper. Set sauce aside. In wok, heat 2 tablespoons oil over medium-high heat. Add catfish. Stir-fry for 4 to 5 minutes, or until fish is firm and opaque and just begins to flake. Remove fish from wok. Place on serving platter. Cover to keep warm. Set aside.

Drain and discard cooking liquid. To same wok, add remaining 1 tablespoon oil. Heat over medium-high heat. Add pea pods and cabbage. Stir-fry for 3 to 4 minutes, or until vegetables are tender-crisp. Add fish and sauce. Stir-fry over medium-high heat for 1½ to 2½ minutes, or until sauce is thickened and translucent, stirring constantly. Garnish with orange slices. Serve over hot cooked rice, if desired.

Per Serving: Calories: 446 • Protein: 49 g. • Carbohydrate: 12 g. • Fat: 21 g. • Cholesterol: 148 mg. • Sodium: 734 mg.
Exchanges: 6½ lean meat, 1¾ vegetable, ¼ fruit

← Oriental-style Fried Fish

Jerry L. Smalley – Columbia Falls, Montana

1½ lbs. sunfish, or substitute, fillets (2 to 3 oz. each), cut into 1-inch pieces
¼ teaspoon salt
¼ teaspoon pepper
¼ teaspoon ground ginger
Vegetable oil

BATTER:
½ cup all-purpose flour
¼ cup water
1 egg, beaten
¼ teaspoon salt

SAUCE:
1 can (11½ oz.) tomato juice
3 tablespoons vinegar
3 tablespoons sugar
1 tablespoon vegetable oil
1 teaspoon ground ginger
¼ teaspoon red pepper sauce
1 tablespoon plus 1½ teaspoons cornstarch mixed with ¼ cup cold water

4 servings

Heat oven to 175°F. Sprinkle fish with salt, pepper and ginger. Set aside. In deep-fat fryer, heat 2 inches oil to 375°F. In medium mixing bowl, combine batter ingredients. Dip fish in batter to coat. In hot oil, fry fish, a few pieces at a time, for 3 to 4 minutes, or until golden brown, turning over once. Drain on paper-towel-lined plate. Place in oven to keep warm.

In 1-quart saucepan, combine all sauce ingredients, except cornstarch mixture. Bring sauce mixture to a boil over medium heat, stirring constantly. Stir cornstarch mixture into sauce mixture. Cook for 30 seconds to 1 minute, or until sauce is thickened and translucent, stirring constantly. Spoon sauce over fish. Serve over hot cooked rice and sprinkle evenly with diagonally sliced green onions, if desired.

Per Serving: Calories: 391 • Protein: 37 g. • Carbohydrate: 29 g. • Fat: 14 g. • Cholesterol: 167 mg. • Sodium: 748 mg.
Exchanges: 1¼ starch, 4½ lean meat, ¾ fruit

Northern Pike Stir-fry →

Karen Bone – Fairbanks, Alaska

2 tablespoons olive or sesame oil
1 small onion, cut into 16 wedges
3 medium carrots, cut into 2 × ¼-inch strips
2 cups broccoli flowerets and pieces
3 cups shredded green cabbage
2 cups flaked cooked northern pike or substitute
1 cup sliced almonds, toasted
2 tablespoons soy sauce

4 servings

In wok, heat oil over medium-high heat. Add onion. Stir-fry for 1 minute, or until tender-crisp. Continue to add vegetables in order given, stir-frying for 1 to 1½ minutes each, or until tender-crisp. Add fish and almonds. Stir-fry for 1 to 1½ minutes, or until hot. Stir in soy sauce. Serve over hot cooked rice or Oriental noodles, if desired.

Per Serving: Calories: 339 • Protein: 28 g. • Carbohydrate: 16 g. • Fat: 20 g. • Cholesterol: 39 mg. • Sodium: 590 mg. Exchanges: 3 lean meat, 3 vegetable, 2 fat

Chinese Fried Rice

Michael DeRose – Talent, Oregon

¼ cup peanut oil
3 cups cold cooked white rice
2 cups any flaked cooked freshwater fish
1 cup fresh snow pea pods
¾ cup coarsely chopped green cabbage
½ cup coarsely chopped red pepper (¾-inch chunks)
½ cup broccoli flowerets
¼ cup carrot strips (2 × ¼-inch strips)
2 tablespoons diagonally sliced green onion
    (2-inch lengths)
3 eggs, beaten
2 teaspoons garlic powder
3 tablespoons soy sauce

4 servings

In wok, heat oil over high heat. Add rice, fish and vegetables. Stir-fry for 5 to 6 minutes, or until mixture is hot and vegetables brighten in color.

Reduce heat to medium-high. Make well in center of rice mixture. Add eggs and garlic powder. Cook for 1 to 1½ minutes, or until eggs begin to set, stirring constantly to scramble. (Eggs should be soft-set.) Add soy sauce. Stir eggs into rice and vegetable mixture.

Per Serving: Calories: 437 • Protein: 29 g. • Carbohydrate: 37 g. • Fat: 18 g. • Cholesterol: 198 mg. • Sodium: 869 mg. Exchanges: 1¾ starch, 2¾ lean meat, 2 vegetable, 2 fat

Techniques for Poaching & Steaming

These cooking methods do not require the addition of fat, so they are among the healthiest ways to prepare fish.

Poaching means cooking the fish by immersing it in liquid heated to just below the boiling point. Poaching works especially well with oily fish because some of the fat leaches out into the cooking liquid.

Steaming means cooking the fish on a rack placed just above boiling liquid. With this technique, the fish are more likely to retain their natural flavor, shape and texture.

The poaching or steaming liquid could be plain water; but wine, vinegar, lemon, apple or orange juice or various vegetables, herbs and spices are normally added to enhance the flavor. If you plan to use the liquid to flavor a soup or sauce, use a *bouquet garni* or seasoning bundle (p. 42), so you won't have to strain out the herbs and spices. You can also poach or steam using Court Bouillon (p. 42) or milk. Poached fish are more likely to absorb flavor from the cooking liquid than are steamed fish.

When using an acidic liquid (such as vinegar or wine) for poaching or steaming, be sure to use cookware made of or lined with nonreactive material such as stainless steel, porcelain enamel, tin or glass. Don't use aluminum cookware unless it is coated or anodized.

HERBS AND SPICES for poaching and steaming include (1) fresh parsley, (2) coriander, (3) fresh marjoram, (4) peppercorns, (5) stick cinnamon, (6) fresh thyme, (7) whole allspice, (8) mustard seed, (9) fresh oregano, (10) whole cloves and (11) fresh rosemary.

FRESH VEGETABLES for poaching and steaming include (1) leeks, (2) carrots, (3) celery, (4) onions and (5) garlic. You can also add slices of fresh citrus fruit or citrus peel.

EQUIPMENT for poaching includes (1) roasting pan; (2) fish poacher, which has a rack with handles for removing fish from the liquid; (3) saucepan and (4) skillet, which are normally used for smaller fish and a (5) long-bladed spatula, for removing smaller fish from the liquid.

You can also use roasting pans, skillets and saucepans for steaming with the addition of a (6) steamer basket or rack that elevates the fish above the liquid. A (7) wok or (8) electric frying pan can also be used for steaming by adding a rack.

Court Bouillon

The Hunting & Fishing Library

 1 leek, cut in half lengthwise and
    rinsed
 4 sprigs fresh parsley
 3 to 4 sprigs fresh thyme
 1 large bay leaf
 1 large clove garlic, cut in half
12 cups water
 2 medium carrots, thinly sliced
 2 ribs celery, thinly sliced
 2 slices lemon

12 cups

Prepare bouquet garni (seasoning bundle) as directed below. Set aside. Place water in stockpot or fish poacher. Add bouquet garni, carrots, celery and lemon. Cover. Bring to a boil over medium-high heat. Reduce heat to low. Simmer for 15 minutes. Add whole fish, fillets or steaks. Cook, covered, for 9 to 11 minutes per inch thickness, or until fish is firm and opaque and just begins to flake.

Nutritional information not available.

How to Prepare Bouquet Garni

CUT two 4-inch pieces from outer layer of halved and rinsed leek. Wrap and refrigerate remaining leek for future use. Place parsley, thyme, bay leaf and garlic on concave side of 1 piece of leek.

COVER with remaining piece of leek. Tie in 3 places with string to secure seasoning bundle.

42

Summer-spiced →
Tomato Pepper Sauce

"This sauce is excellent served over mild-tasting fish."
    Vicki J. Snyder – Columbus, Ohio

1 medium tomato, peeled, seeded
     and chopped (1 cup)
½ cup finely chopped yellow
     pepper
½ cup finely chopped green pepper
½ cup finely chopped red onion
1 tablespoon finely chopped
     pickled hot chili peppers
1 teaspoon fresh lemon juice
1 teaspoon red wine vinegar
1 clove garlic, minced
¼ teaspoon salt

8 servings

In medium mixing bowl, combine
all ingredients. Cover with plastic
wrap. Chill at least 2 hours. Serve
with poached, fried or baked fish.
Store, covered, in refrigerator no
longer than 1 week.

Per Serving: Calories: 12 • Protein: 1 g.
• Carbohydrate: 3 g. • Fat: 0
• Cholesterol: 0 • Sodium: 86 mg.
Exchanges: ½ vegetable

Mustard Sauce Dijon

*"Excellent with Lake Erie perch and
walleye, as an alternative to tartar sauce."*
    Brenda L. Novak – Westfield Center, Ohio

⅓ cup Dijon mustard
¼ cup vegetable oil
2 tablespoons sugar
1 teaspoon snipped fresh parsley
1 teaspoon snipped fresh chives
1 teaspoon white wine vinegar
1 clove garlic, minced

4 servings

In medium mixing bowl, combine
all ingredients. Mix well with whisk.
Serve with poached, fried or baked
fish. Store, covered, in refrigerator
no longer than 1 week.

Per Serving: Calories: 170 • Protein: 0
• Carbohydrate: 9 g. • Fat: 15 g.
• Cholesterol: 0 • Sodium: 594 mg.
Exchanges: ⅔ fruit, 3 fat

Morel Mushroom Sauce ↑

The Hunting & Fishing Library

½ oz. dried morel mushrooms
1 cup boiling water
2 tablespoons margarine or butter
¼ cup sliced green onions
2 tablespoons all-purpose flour

¼ teaspoon salt
¼ teaspoon ground ginger
⅛ teaspoon pepper
¾ cup half-and-half
1 tablespoon dry sherry

4 servings

In medium mixing bowl, combine mushrooms and boiling water. Let stand
for 30 minutes to rehydrate. Drain, reserving ½ cup of soaking liquid.
Coarsely chop morels. Set aside.

In 2-quart saucepan, melt margarine over medium heat. Add onions and
mushrooms. Cook for 2 minutes, or until vegetables are tender, stirring constantly. Stir in flour, salt, ginger and pepper. Blend in reserved morel liquid
and the half-and-half.

Cook over medium heat, stirring constantly, until mixture thickens and
bubbles. Stir in sherry. Serve with poached or baked fish.

Per Serving: Calories: 142 • Protein: 2 g. • Carbohydrate: 8 g. • Fat: 11 g.
• Cholesterol: 17 mg. • Sodium: 222 mg.
Exchanges: ⅓ starch, ½ vegetable, ¼ skim milk, 2 fat

Tomato Caper Sauced Trout

Richard J. Parmley – St. Louis, Missouri

12 cups water
1 medium onion, thinly sliced
1 carrot, thinly sliced
3 thin slices lemon
2 whole drawn stream trout
   (8 oz. each)

SAUCE:
½ cup seeded chopped tomato
¼ cup olive oil
3 tablespoons snipped fresh basil
   leaves
2 tablespoons dry white wine
1 tablespoon capers
1 clove garlic, minced
⅛ teaspoon salt
⅛ teaspoon pepper

2 servings

In fish poacher, combine water, onion, carrot and lemon. Cover. Bring to a boil over medium-high heat. Add fish. Reduce heat to low. Simmer, covered, for 8 to 10 minutes, or until fish begins to flake when fork is inserted at backbone in thickest part of fish.

Drain and discard poaching liquid. Cool fish slightly. Carefully remove heads and skin. Cut through backbones to make 4 fillets. Place in 11 × 7-inch baking dish or deep serving platter.

In medium mixing bowl, combine sauce ingredients. Spoon over fish. Cover with plastic wrap. Marinate in refrigerator at least 15 minutes. Serve chilled.

Per Serving: Calories: 423 • Protein: 28 g. • Carbohydrate: 4 g. • Fat: 32 g. • Cholesterol: 76 mg. • Sodium: 290 mg. Exchanges: 4 lean meat, ¾ vegetable, 3¾ fat

Poached Whole Salmon ↑ with Cucumber & Fennel Hollandaise

Darina Allen – Ballymaloe Cookery School, Shanagarry, Co. Cork, Ireland

16 cups water
2 tablespoons salt
1 whole drawn salmon or
   substitute (2¾ to 3¼ lbs.)
2 teaspoons butter
½ cup peeled seeded chopped
   cucumber
2 egg yolks
2 teaspoons cold water

½ cup cold butter, cut into 16 pieces
1 teaspoon lemon juice
1 teaspoon snipped fresh fennel
   leaves

GARNISH:
   Parsley
   Lemon balm
   Fennel
10 to 12 wedges lemon

6 servings

In fish poacher, combine water and salt. Bring to a boil over medium-high heat. Place salmon on rack. Add to poacher. Reduce heat to low. Simmer, covered, for 20 minutes. Remove poacher from heat. Leave salmon in poaching liquid for 20 to 30 minutes.

In 8-inch skillet, melt 2 teaspoons butter over medium heat. Add cucumber. Cook for 1 to 2 minutes, or until hot, stirring constantly. Remove from heat. Set aside. Prepare hollandaise sauce as directed opposite.

Carefully lift poaching rack out of poacher. Let fish drain on rack for a few minutes. Slide fish onto large serving platter. Garnish with parsley, lemon balm, fennel and lemon wedges. Just before serving, remove skin from salmon. Remove all fish from top of salmon, then delicately remove bone and continue serving from bottom. Spoon sauce evenly over each serving.

Per Serving: Calories: 359 • Protein: 28 g. • Carbohydrate: 1 g. • Fat: 27 g. • Cholesterol: 189 mg. • Sodium: 644 mg. Exchanges: 4 lean meat, 3 fat

How to Prepare Hollandaise Sauce

COMBINE egg yolks and 2 teaspoons water in heavy 1-quart saucepan. Beat well with whisk. Place pan over very low heat. (You should be able to put your hand on side of saucepan at any time during cooking.)

ADD cold butter, 1 piece at a time, beating with whisk after each addition until melted. (If saucepan is too hot for your hand, remove from heat momentarily, but continue beating with whisk and adding butter.)

CONTINUE beating constantly until mixture thickens slightly. Remove from heat. Add juice.

BEAT in cucumber mixture and fennel. Place sauce in bowl over warm water to keep warm.

Poached Panfish with Lemon Chive Sauce

Keith Sutton – Benton, Arkansas

2 cups water
1 bay leaf
¼ teaspoon salt
2 tablespoons lemon juice
1½ lbs. yellow perch, or substitute,
   fillets (2 to 3 oz. each), skin
   removed

SAUCE:
⅓ cup margarine or butter
3 tablespoons snipped fresh chives
½ teaspoon grated lemon peel
¼ teaspoon salt
⅛ teaspoon pepper

4 servings

In 10-inch skillet, combine water, bay leaf, ¼ teaspoon salt and the lemon juice. Bring to a boil over medium-high heat. Add fillets. Reduce heat to low. Simmer, covered, for 3 to 5 minutes, or until fish is firm and opaque and just begins to flake. Drain and discard poaching liquid. Cover fish to keep warm. Set aside.

In 8-inch skillet, melt margarine over medium heat. Add remaining sauce ingredients. Cook for 2 to 3 minutes, or until mixture is hot, stirring constantly. Serve sauce over fish.

Per Serving: Calories: 292 • Protein: 33 g. • Carbohydrate: 1 g. • Fat: 17 g.
• Cholesterol: 153 mg. • Sodium: 487 mg.
Exchanges: 4¾ lean meat, ½ fat

← Walleye Italiano

Ken and Donna White –
Independence, Missouri

3 tablespoons margarine or butter
¾ cup chopped onion
¾ cup chopped green pepper
1 cup tomato juice
1 teaspoon chili powder
¾ teaspoon salt, divided
¼ teaspoon garlic powder
¼ teaspoon dried thyme leaves
¼ teaspoon dried oregano leaves
¼ teaspoon pepper, divided
2 lbs. walleye, or substitute,
   fillets (8 oz. each), skin
   removed
1 cup water
½ cup white wine
1½ cups shredded mozzarella
   cheese

4 to 5 servings

Heat oven to 350°F. In 2-quart saucepan, melt margarine over medium-high heat. Add onion and green pepper. Cook for 4 to 5 minutes, or until vegetables are tender-crisp, stirring constantly. Stir in tomato juice, chili powder, ½ teaspoon salt, the garlic powder, thyme, oregano and ⅛ teaspoon pepper. Bring to a boil. Reduce heat to low. Simmer for 15 to 20 minutes, or until sauce thickens.

Meanwhile, place fillets in deep 10-inch skillet. Sprinkle with remaining ¼ teaspoon salt and ⅛ teaspoon pepper. Pour water and wine over fish. Bring to a boil over medium-high heat. Reduce heat to low. Simmer, covered, for 8 to 10 minutes, or until fish is firm and opaque and just begins to flake.

Drain and discard poaching liquid. Place fillets in 11 × 7-inch baking dish. Spoon warm sauce over fish. Sprinkle evenly with cheese. Bake, uncovered, for 5 to 8 minutes, or until cheese is melted.

Per Serving: Calories: 353 • Protein: 42 g.
• Carbohydrate: 6 g. • Fat: 17 g.
• Cholesterol: 183 mg. • Sodium: 759 mg.
Exchanges: 5½ lean meat, 1 vegetable

Oven-poached Walleye →

"Serve with vegetables or a salad and crusty bread. Low in calories and a good, light meal."

Loretta Conklin – Tuxedo Park, New York

2¼ lbs. walleye, or substitute, fillets
     (6 oz. each), skin removed
½ teaspoon salt
½ teaspoon paprika
¼ teaspoon pepper
1½ cups milk
    Sliced green onions
    Lemon wedges

6 servings

Heat oven to 350°F. Place fillets in 13 × 9-inch baking dish. Sprinkle with salt, paprika and pepper. Pour milk over fish. Cover with foil. Bake for 30 to 35 minutes, or until fish is firm and opaque and just begins to flake.

Lift fillets from poaching liquid. Place on serving platter. Drain and discard poaching liquid. Before serving, sprinkle fish with onions and lemon juice.

Per Serving: Calories: 147 • Protein: 29 g. • Carbohydrate: 1 g. • Fat: 2 g. • Cholesterol: 131 mg. • Sodium: 265 mg. Exchanges: 4 lean meat

Poached Bass with Elegant Sauce

Joan Cone – Williamsburg, Virginia

1 cup water
1 bay leaf
1 teaspoon instant minced onion
1 tablespoon lemon juice
½ teaspoon salt
2 whole drawn bass or substitute
    (1 lb. each)
2 tablespoons margarine or butter,
    divided
¼ cup sliced almonds
4 oz. fresh mushrooms, sliced
    (1 cup)
¼ cup sliced green onions
2 tablespoons all-purpose flour
¼ teaspoon salt
⅛ teaspoon pepper
¾ cup ready-to-serve chicken broth
2 tablespoons dry white wine
2 tablespoons half-and-half

3 servings

In deep 10-inch skillet or electric frying pan, combine water, bay leaf, minced onion, juice and salt. Bring to a boil over medium-high heat. Add bass. Reduce heat to low. Simmer, covered, for 10 to 15 minutes, or until fish begins to flake when fork is inserted at backbone in thickest part of fish. Drain and discard poaching liquid. Cool fish slightly. Carefully remove heads and skin. Cut through backbones to make 4 fillets. Place on serving platter. Cover to keep warm. Set aside.

While fish is poaching, prepare sauce. In 10-inch skillet, melt 1 tablespoon margarine over medium heat. Add almonds. Cook for 2 to 3 minutes, or until light golden brown, stirring constantly. Remove almonds from skillet with slotted spoon. Set aside.

Add remaining 1 tablespoon margarine, the mushrooms and green onions to same skillet. Cook over medium heat for 3 to 4 minutes, or until vegetables are tender-crisp, stirring constantly. Stir in flour, salt and pepper. Blend in broth. Cook until mixture thickens and bubbles, stirring constantly. Stir in wine, half-and-half and almonds. Cook about 30 seconds, or until hot. Serve sauce over fish.

Per Serving: Calories: 309 • Protein: 30 g. • Carbohydrate: 7 g. • Fat: 17 g. • Cholesterol: 122 mg. • Sodium: 805 mg. Exchanges: ¼ starch, 4 lean meat, 1 vegetable, ¾ fat

Chili-sauced Fillets

Wayne A. Hendrickx – Ferndale, Washington

4 slices bacon
¼ cup sliced green onions
3 cloves garlic, minced
1 can (4 oz.) chopped green chilies, undrained
2 tablespoons canned sliced jalapeño peppers, drained and chopped
1 tablespoon chili powder
¼ teaspoon cayenne
2 cans (14½ oz. each) whole tomatoes, undrained and cut up
¼ cup snipped fresh cilantro leaves
2 tablespoons Worcestershire sauce
2 teaspoons sugar
2 teaspoons dried oregano leaves
½ teaspoon ground cumin
2½ lbs. any freshwater fish fillets (8 oz. each), skin on
1 recipe Court Bouillon, page 42

8 to 10 servings

In 6-quart Dutch oven or stockpot, cook bacon over medium heat until brown and crisp. Drain, reserving 2 tablespoons bacon drippings in Dutch oven. Crumble bacon and set aside.

Add onions, garlic, chilies, jalapeño peppers, chili powder and cayenne to drippings in Dutch oven. Cook over medium-high heat for 3 to 5 minutes, or until vegetables are tender-crisp, stirring constantly. Stir in bacon and remaining ingredients, except fillets and Court Bouillon. Bring to a boil over medium-high heat. Reduce heat to low. Simmer for 25 to 30 minutes, or until mixture is very thick, stirring occasionally.

Poach fillets in Court Bouillon as directed. Drain and discard poaching liquid. Serve sauce over fish.

Per Serving: Calories: 226 • Protein: 25 g. • Carbohydrate: 7 g.
• Fat: 11 g. • Cholesterol: 66 mg. • Sodium: 373 mg.
Exchanges: 3 lean meat, 1¼ vegetable, ¼ fat

Salmon Pasta Salad →

Vicki J. Snyder – Columbus, Ohio

2 salmon, or substitute, steaks
    (8 oz. each), 1 inch thick
1 recipe Court Bouillon, page 42
1 pkg. (12 oz.) uncooked mini
    lasagna noodles
1 cup thinly sliced carrots
1 tablespoon olive oil
½ cup thinly sliced celery
½ cup sliced green onions
½ cup chopped green pepper
¼ cup pine nuts, toasted
½ cup mayonnaise
½ cup ranch salad dressing
¼ teaspoon salt
⅛ teaspoon pepper
1 medium tomato, seeded and
    chopped (1 cup)
½ cup sliced black olives

6 servings

Poach salmon in Court Bouillon as directed. Drain and discard poaching liquid. Chill salmon 2 hours. Remove skin and bones; flake meat. Set aside.

Prepare mini lasagna as directed on package, adding carrots to boiling water during last 1 minute of cooking time. Rinse pasta and carrots with cold water. Drain. Place in large mixing bowl or salad bowl. Add oil. Toss to coat. Add celery, onions, green pepper, salmon and pine nuts. Mix well.

In small mixing bowl, combine mayonnaise, ranch dressing, salt and pepper. Add mayonnaise mixture to pasta mixture, stirring gently to coat. Serve immediately or cover and chill until serving time. Top each serving evenly with tomatoes and olives.

Per Serving: Calories: 623 • Protein: 23 g.
• Carbohydrate: 50 g. • Fat: 37 g.
• Cholesterol: 53 mg. • Sodium: 552 mg.
Exchanges: 3 starch, 2 lean meat,
1 vegetable, 5¾ fat

Cocktail Perch

"This fish is also good served warm with tartar sauce. When warm, it tastes remarkably like lobster."
Adell Carr Smith – Battlefield, Missouri

12 cups water
2 tablespoons salt
2 slices lemon

1 lb. yellow perch, or substitute, fillets (2 to 3 oz. each), skin removed, cut into 3 × ½-inch strips
    Crushed ice
    Seafood cocktail sauce

6 servings

In 6-quart Dutch oven or stockpot, combine water, salt and lemon. Bring to a boil over high heat. Reduce heat to medium. Add perch strips. Cook, uncovered, for 3 to 4 minutes, or until fish is firm and opaque and just begins to curl up. Lift fish strips from poaching liquid and plunge immediately into ice water. Leave fish in ice water until completely cooled. Serve fish strips on bed of crushed ice with cocktail sauce.

Per Serving: Calories: 69 • Protein: 15 g. • Carbohydrate: 0 • Fat: 1 g.
• Cholesterol: 68 mg. • Sodium: 414 mg.
Exchanges: 2 lean meat

King of the Sea Primavera

"Great for those watching fat intake."
Gloria Rose – Springfield, New Jersey

2 salmon, or substitute, steaks
   (8 oz. each), 1 inch thick
1 recipe Court Bouillon, page 42
1/3 cup dry white wine
12 oz. uncooked whole wheat
   spaghetti
4 cups fresh broccoli flowerets
1 medium red pepper, cut into
   thin strips
1 cup prepared marinara sauce
1/3 cup low-fat buttermilk
8 oz. fresh mushrooms, cut into
   quarters (2 cups)
2 tablespoons shredded fresh
   Parmesan cheese (optional)

6 servings

Poach salmon in Court Bouillon as directed. Drain and discard poaching liquid. Place salmon in medium mixing bowl. Pour wine over salmon. Cover with plastic wrap. Chill salmon 2 hours. Remove skin and bones; flake meat. Set aside.

Prepare spaghetti as directed on package, adding broccoli and red pepper to boiling water during last 3 minutes of cooking time. Rinse pasta and vegetables with hot water. Drain. Cover to keep warm. Set aside.

In 1-quart saucepan, combine marinara sauce and buttermilk. Cook over low heat (do not boil) until hot.

In large mixing bowl or salad bowl, combine pasta mixture, mushrooms and salmon. Add marinara sauce mixture. Toss gently to coat. Sprinkle with Parmesan cheese.

Per Serving: Calories: 373 • Protein: 26 g. • Carbohydrate: 55 g. • Fat: 7 g.
• Cholesterol: 37 mg. • Sodium: 333 mg.
Exchanges: 3 starch, 2 lean meat, 2 vegetable, 1/4 fat

Bass au Gratin

Annette Bignami – Moscow, Idaho

1½ lbs. bass, or substitute, fillets
    (6 oz. each), skin removed
1 recipe Court Bouillon, page 42
¼ cup margarine or butter, divided
3 tablespoons all-purpose flour
¼ teaspoon salt
¼ teaspoon dry mustard
⅛ teaspoon pepper
2 cups milk
¾ cup shredded Swiss cheese
¼ cup sliced green onions
1 teaspoon dried bouquet garni
    seasoning
¼ cup crushed cracker crumbs

4 to 6 servings

Poach bass fillets in Court Bouillon as directed. Drain and discard poaching liquid. Cool fish slightly. Remove skin and bones; flake meat. Set aside.

Heat oven to 350°F. Grease 9-inch square baking dish. Set aside. In 2-quart saucepan, melt 3 tablespoons margarine over medium heat. Stir in flour, salt, dry mustard and pepper. Blend in milk. Cook, stirring constantly, over medium heat until mixture thickens and bubbles. Remove from heat. Stir in cheese until melted. Stir in onions, bouquet garni and flaked fish. Spoon mixture into prepared dish.

In 1-quart saucepan, melt remaining 1 tablespoon margarine over low heat. Stir in cracker crumbs. Sprinkle crumb mixture over fish mixture. Bake for 20 to 25 minutes, or until hot and bubbly around edges. Let stand for 5 minutes before serving.

Per Serving: Calories: 333 • Protein: 29 g. • Carbohydrate: 12 g. • Fat: 18 g. • Cholesterol: 102 mg. • Sodium: 336 mg. Exchanges: ½ starch, 3½ lean meat, ⅓ skim milk, 1½ fat

Salmon Salad Sandwiches ↑

Vicki J. Snyder – Columbus, Ohio

2 salmon, or substitute, steaks
    (8 oz. each), 1 inch thick
1 recipe Court Bouillon, page 42
2 hard-cooked eggs, chopped
½ cup mayonnaise
2 tablespoons sliced green onion
2 tablespoons sweet pickle relish
1 teaspoon lemon juice
½ teaspoon hot pepper sauce
¼ teaspoon salt
⅛ teaspoon pepper
4 to 6 thick slices crusty bread
    Leaf lettuce

4 to 6 servings

Poach salmon in Court Bouillon as directed. Drain and discard poaching liquid. Chill salmon 2 hours. Remove skin and bones; flake meat.

In medium mixing bowl, combine salmon and remaining ingredients, except bread and lettuce. Cover with plastic wrap. Chill about 1 hour. Serve on bread with lettuce.

Per Serving: Calories: 260 • Protein: 16 g. • Carbohydrate: 3 g. • Fat: 21 g. • Cholesterol: 118 mg. • Sodium: 292 mg. Exchanges: 2 lean meat, ½ vegetable, 3 fat

Bass Enchiladas

Annette Bignami – Moscow, Idaho

1 lb. bass, or substitute, fillets (8 oz. each), skin removed
1 recipe Court Bouillon, page 42
1 cup chopped onions
½ cup water
1 can (10 oz.) mild enchilada sauce
1 can (10 oz.) hot enchilada sauce
2 cups shredded Cheddar cheese, divided
¾ cup sliced black olives, divided
3 hard-cooked eggs, chopped, divided
1 can (4 oz.) chopped green chilies, drained
8 flour tortillas (8-inch)
1 cup shredded Monterey Jack cheese

6 to 8 servings

Poach bass fillets in Court Bouillon as directed. Drain and discard poaching liquid. Cool fish slightly. Remove skin and bones; flake meat. Set aside.

Heat oven to 350°F. In 8-inch skillet, combine onions and water. Bring to a boil over medium-high heat. Reduce heat to low and simmer for 3 minutes. Remove from heat. Drain. Set onions aside. In same skillet, combine mild and hot enchilada sauces. Cook over medium heat until hot. In medium mixing bowl, combine fish, onions, 1 cup Cheddar cheese, ½ cup olives, 2 chopped eggs and the chilies.

To assemble enchiladas, dip each tortilla in warm sauce. Place in 13 × 9-inch baking dish. Spoon ½ cup fish mixture down center of each tortilla and roll up. Pour remaining sauce over enchiladas. Cover dish with foil. Bake for 30 to 35 minutes, or until hot and bubbly around edges. Remove foil. Sprinkle enchiladas with remaining Cheddar cheese and the Monterey Jack cheese. Top with remaining olives and egg. Re-cover. Bake for 5 to 10 minutes, or until cheeses are melted.

Per Serving: Calories: 428 • Protein: 28 g. • Carbohydrate: 35 g. • Fat: 19 g.
• Cholesterol: 160 mg. • Sodium: 1402 mg.
Exchanges: 2 starch, 3 lean meat, 1 vegetable, 2 fat

Northwest Salmon Burritos

Lyle Gabel – Bismarck, North Dakota

1 salmon, or substitute, steak
   (8 oz.), 1 inch thick
1 recipe Court Bouillon, page 42
1 can (4½ oz.) small shrimp,
   rinsed and drained
1 can (4 oz.) chopped green chilies,
   drained
2 cups shredded Cheddar cheese,
   divided
½ cup seeded chopped tomato
¼ cup sliced green onions
½ teaspoon chili powder
1 tablespoon lemon juice
8 flour tortillas (8-inch)

SAUCE:
2 tablespoons margarine or butter
2 tablespoons all-purpose flour
¼ teaspoon salt
1 cup milk
1 cup shredded Monterey Jack
   cheese

4 servings

Poach salmon in Court Bouillon as directed. Drain and discard poaching liquid. Cool salmon slightly. Remove skin and bones; flake meat.

Heat oven to 350°F. In medium mixing bowl, combine salmon, shrimp, green chilies, 1 cup Cheddar cheese, the tomato, onions, chili powder and juice. Spoon about ½ cup salmon mixture down center of each tortilla. Roll up tortillas and place in 13 × 9-inch baking dish. Cover with foil. Bake for 30 minutes. Remove foil and sprinkle with remaining 1 cup Cheddar cheese. Re-cover and bake for 5 to 8 minutes, or until cheese is melted.

While burritos are baking, prepare sauce. In 2-quart saucepan, melt margarine over medium heat. Stir in flour and salt. Blend in milk. Cook, stirring constantly, until mixture thickens and bubbles. Remove from heat. Add Monterey Jack cheese. Stir until cheese is melted. Serve burritos with sauce. Garnish with chopped fresh tomato and sliced green onions, if desired.

Per Serving: Calories: 789 • Protein: 48 g. • Carbohydrate: 58 g. • Fat: 40 g.
• Cholesterol: 176 mg. • Sodium: 1409 mg.
Exchanges: 3 starch, 5½ lean meat, 1 vegetable, ¼ skim milk, 4½ fat

Perch Thermidor ↑

Peggy S. Day – Boerne, Texas

1 lb. yellow perch, or substitute, fillets (2 to 3 oz. each), skin removed
1 recipe Court Bouillon, page 42
1 pkg. (10 oz.) frozen puff pastry shells
3 tablespoons margarine or butter
¼ cup chopped red pepper
¼ cup chopped green pepper
3 tablespoons all-purpose flour
½ teaspoon seasoned salt
⅛ teaspoon pepper
1½ cups milk
1 cup shredded Cheddar cheese
1 tablespoon dry sherry
Paprika

6 servings

Poach perch in Court Bouillon as directed. Drain and discard poaching liquid. Cool perch slightly. Remove bones; flake meat. Set aside.

Bake puff pastry shells as directed on package. In 2-quart saucepan, melt margarine over medium-low heat. Add peppers. Cook for 3 to 4 minutes, or until peppers are tender-crisp, stirring constantly. Stir in flour, seasoned salt and pepper. Blend in milk.

Cook for 6 to 8 minutes, or until mixture thickens and bubbles, stirring constantly. Remove from heat. Stir in Cheddar cheese until melted. Stir in sherry and perch. Spoon about ½ cup fish mixture over each pastry shell. Sprinkle each with paprika.

Per Serving: Calories: 464 • Protein: 25 g. • Carbohydrate: 23 g. • Fat: 30 g.
• Cholesterol: 96 mg. • Sodium: 543 mg.
Exchanges: 1½ starch, 3 lean meat, 4 fat

Crayfish Curry

Thomas K. Squier – Aberdeen, North Carolina

¼ cup margarine or butter
½ cup chopped onion
½ cup chopped green pepper
1 clove garlic, minced
2 tablespoons curry powder
½ cup cream of coconut
½ cup chopped fresh or canned mango
1 lb. steamed peeled crayfish tails
Hot cooked rice

4 servings

In 6-quart Dutch oven or stockpot, melt margarine over medium heat. Add onion, green pepper and garlic. Cook for 3 to 4 minutes, or until vegetables are tender-crisp, stirring constantly. Add curry powder. Cook for 3 minutes, stirring constantly. Stir in cream of coconut, mango and crayfish. Cook for 4 to 5 minutes, or until hot. Serve over rice.

Per Serving: Calories: 337 • Protein: 29 g.
• Carbohydrate: 11 g. • Fat: 20 g.
• Cholesterol: 202 mg. • Sodium: 232 mg.
Exchanges: 4 lean meat, ½ vegetable, ½ fruit, 1½ fat

Chinese-style Steamed Trout ↑

Richard J. Parmley – St. Louis, Missouri

2 whole drawn stream trout
   (8 oz. each)
1 tablespoon grated fresh
   gingerroot
1 tablespoon minced garlic
1 tablespoon fermented Chinese
   black beans
4 chopsticks
2 tablespoons soy sauce
2 tablespoons dry white wine
2 green onions, cut diagonally
   into 2 × ⅛-inch strips
1 medium carrot, cut into
   2 × ⅛-inch strips

2 servings

Per Serving: Calories: 214 • Protein: 31 g.
• Carbohydrate: 8 g. • Fat: 5 g.
• Cholesterol: 80 mg. • Sodium: 1042 mg.
Exchanges: 4 lean meat, 1 vegetable

How to Prepare Chinese-style Steamed Trout

HEAT oven to 400°F. Using razor blade or very sharp knife, score both sides of each trout in crisscross pattern, with cuts approximately ¼ inch deep and ½ inch apart.

COMBINE gingerroot, garlic and black beans in small mixing bowl. Place 1 teaspoon gingerroot mixture in cavity of each fish.

ARRANGE chopsticks crosswise in 13 × 9-inch baking dish. Place trout on chopsticks. Spoon soy sauce over fish. Top each fish with remaining ginger mixture. Pour wine in bottom of dish.

CRISSCROSS onion and carrot strips on each fish. Cover dish with foil. Bake for 12 to 14 minutes, or until fish begins to flake when fork is inserted at backbone in thickest part of fish.

Pot Stickers

*"Pot stickers work more than one way!
You can serve them as entrées or snacks,
cook them in the skillet, steam or boil
them, or even serve them in soup. They
also freeze well."*
  Annette Bignami – Moscow, Idaho

1/4 cup chopped water chestnuts
  2 shallots, finely chopped
  2 tablespoons snipped fresh parsley
  1 teaspoon sesame oil
1/4 teaspoon salt
1/4 teaspoon pepper
1 1/2 lbs. bass, or substitute, fillets
      (6 oz. each), cut into 1-inch
      pieces
  2 tablespoons sherry
 15 eggroll skins (7-inch square)
  1 egg, beaten
  1 cup water
  2 tablespoons vegetable oil

4 to 5 servings

In medium mixing bowl, combine
water chestnuts, shallots, parsley,
sesame oil, salt and pepper. Set
aside. In food processor, combine
fish and sherry. Pulse 5 or 6 times,
or until finely chopped. Add to
vegetable mixture. Mix well. Assemble as directed below.

In 12-inch nonstick skillet with
cover, heat water and vegetable
oil until boiling. Add pot stickers.
Reduce heat to medium-low.
Cover. Cook for 10 minutes. Remove cover. Cook for 4 to 6 minutes longer, or until water boils
off and bottoms are golden brown.
Serve with mixture of teriyaki
sauce and sliced green onions,
or with dip made to taste from
prepared mustard, soy sauce and
catsup, if desired.

Per Serving: Calories: 465 • Protein: 37 g.
• Carbohydrate: 47 g. • Fat: 13 g.
• Cholesterol: 135 mg. • Sodium: 240 mg.
Exchanges: 2¾ starch, 4 lean meat,
1 vegetable, ¼ fat

How to Assemble Pot Stickers

CUT 6-inch circle from each eggroll
skin. (Use inverted 1 1/2 pint mixing
bowl as template.) Cover eggroll skins
with plastic wrap to prevent drying.
Place 2 level tablespoons filling
mixture on half of 1 circle, 1/4 inch
from edge.

BRUSH edges lightly with egg. Fold
other half over, pressing with fingers
to seal. Bring long corners together,
overlapping slightly. Brush lightly with
egg to seal. Keep pot stickers covered.
Repeat with remaining filling and
eggroll circles.

56

Salmon Pâté ↑

Wayne Phillips – Saskatoon, Saskatchewan

1 salmon, or substitute, steak
(8 oz.), 1 inch thick
1 recipe Court Bouillon, page 42
1/3 cup snipped fresh parsley
1/4 cup sliced green onions
1 clove garlic, minced
4 oz. cream cheese, softened
2 tablespoons margarine or
butter, softened
1/2 teaspoon dried thyme leaves
1/4 teaspoon salt
1/8 teaspoon pepper

1 1/2 cups, 12 servings

Poach salmon in Court Bouillon as
directed. Drain and discard poaching liquid. Cool salmon slightly.
Remove skin and bones; flake
meat. Set aside.

In food processor, combine parsley,
onions and garlic. Process until
finely chopped. Add cream cheese,
margarine, thyme, salt and pepper.
Process until smooth. Stir in salmon.

Spoon into small soufflé dish or
2-cup serving dish. Cover with plastic wrap. Refrigerate several hours
or overnight. Serve as a spread with
crackers or celery and carrot sticks,
if desired.

Per Serving: Calories: 75 • Protein: 4 g.
• Carbohydrate: 1 g. • Fat: 6 g.
• Cholesterol: 20 mg. • Sodium: 104 mg.
Exchanges: 1/2 lean meat, 1 fat

Salmon Vegetable Dip ↑

"This is my original recipe."
Yolan Rakityan – Cleveland, Ohio

2 salmon, or substitute, steaks
(8 oz. each), 1 inch thick
1 recipe Court Bouillon, page 42
3/4 cup salad dressing or
mayonnaise
1/2 cup sliced green onions
1/2 cup sour cream
1 pkg. (1.4 oz.) dry vegetable
soup and recipe mix

2 1/2 cups, 20 servings

Poach salmon in Court Bouillon
as directed. Drain and discard
poaching liquid. Chill salmon 2
hours. Remove skin and bones;
flake meat.

In medium mixing bowl, combine
salmon and remaining ingredients.
Cover with plastic wrap. Refrigerate several hours or overnight.
Serve as a spread with crackers
or celery and carrot sticks, if desired.

Per Serving: Calories: 82 • Protein: 5 g.
• Carbohydrate: 4 g. • Fat: 5 g.
• Cholesterol: 16 mg. • Sodium: 185 mg.
Exchanges: 1/2 lean meat, 3/4 vegetable,
3/4 fat

Party Trout Dip ↑

Geri and Larry Harkness –
Murfreesboro, Tennessee

2 whole drawn stream trout
(8 oz. each)
1 recipe Court Bouillon, page 42
12 oz. cream cheese, softened
1 cup sour cream
1/2 cup sliced green onions
1/3 cup salad dressing or
mayonnaise
3 tablespoons dried parsley flakes
1 jar (2 oz.) diced pimiento, drained
1/4 teaspoon salt
1/8 teaspoon pepper

4 cups, 32 servings

Poach trout in Court Bouillon as
directed. Drain and discard poaching liquid. Cool trout slightly. Remove heads, skin and bones; flake
meat. Set aside.

In medium mixing bowl, combine
cream cheese, sour cream, onions,
salad dressing, parsley flakes,
pimiento, salt and pepper. Stir in
trout. Cover with plastic wrap.
Refrigerate several hours or overnight. Serve as a spread with
crackers or celery and carrot sticks,
if desired.

Per Serving: Calories: 73 • Protein: 3 g.
• Carbohydrate: 1 g. • Fat: 6 g.
• Cholesterol: 20 mg. • Sodium: 72 mg.
Exchanges: 1/3 lean meat, 1/4 vegetable,
1 fat

Simmering & Stewing

Techniques for Simmering & Stewing

These techniques involve cooking at temperatures just below the boiling point (or about 185°F). You'll know the temperature is right when tiny bubbles rise to the surface.

Simmering is used to prepare soups, chowders, bouillabaisse and gumbo. Stewing usually requires a longer cooking time, tenderizing tough meats (such as snapping turtle) and giving the flavors a better chance to blend.

You can garnish soups and stews with one or more of the following: shredded cheese, seasoned croutons, sour cream, snipped fresh herbs, popcorn, pretzels and sliced green onions.

←Northwoods Minestrone

The Hunting & Fishing Library

2 tablespoons olive oil
½ cup sliced green onions
½ cup chopped red or green pepper
2 cans (28 oz. each) whole tomatoes, undrained and cut up
½ cup water
2 teaspoons sugar
1 teaspoon Italian seasoning
½ teaspoon salt
¼ teaspoon garlic powder
⅛ to ¼ teaspoon cayenne
1½ lbs. walleye, or substitute, fillets (6 oz. each), skin removed, cut into 1½-inch pieces
1 can (15½ oz.) dark red kidney beans, rinsed and drained
1 pkg. (9 oz.) frozen Italian or cut green beans
1 cup uncooked rotini

6 to 8 servings

In 6-quart Dutch oven or stockpot, heat oil over medium-high heat. Add onions and chopped pepper. Cook for 3 to 5 minutes, or until vegetables are tender, stirring constantly.

Stir in tomatoes, water, sugar, Italian seasoning, salt, garlic powder and cayenne. Bring to a boil. Reduce heat to low. Simmer for 5 minutes.

Stir in remaining ingredients. Return mixture to a boil over medium-high heat. Reduce heat to low. Simmer for 15 to 20 minutes, or until fish is firm and opaque and just begins to flake, stirring occasionally.

Per Serving: Calories: 242 • Protein: 21 g. • Carbohydrate: 29 g. • Fat: 5 g. • Cholesterol: 61 mg. • Sodium: 569 mg.
Exchanges: 1 starch, 2 lean meat, 2 vegetable

Crayfish Creole

Arthur H. Pratt – Stone Mountain, Georgia

⅓ cup shortening
¼ cup all-purpose flour
1 can (28 oz.) whole tomatoes, undrained and cut up
1 cup chopped onions
1 cup sliced green onions
1 cup water
½ cup chopped green pepper
½ cup chopped celery
1 tablespoon Worcestershire sauce
2 cloves garlic, minced
1 teaspoon hot pepper sauce
½ teaspoon salt
¼ teaspoon pepper
⅛ teaspoon cayenne
1½ to 2 lbs. steamed peeled crayfish tails

4 to 6 servings

In 6-quart Dutch oven or stockpot, melt shortening over medium heat. Add flour. Cook for 5 to 8 minutes, stirring constantly, until dark golden brown. Remove from heat.

Add remaining ingredients, except crayfish. Bring to a boil. Reduce heat to low. Simmer, covered, for 30 minutes. Add crayfish. Cook for 4 to 6 minutes, or until mixture is hot. Serve over hot cooked rice, if desired.

Per Serving: Calories: 317 • Protein: 34 g. • Carbohydrate: 14 g. • Fat: 14 g. • Cholesterol: 236 mg. • Sodium: 548 mg.
Exchanges: ¼ starch, 4 lean meat, 2 vegetable, ½ fat

Bluegills Bouillabaisse à la Jack Frost

Jack Frost – Round Lake, Illinois

¼ cup olive oil
1 cup chopped onions
1 cup chopped red pepper
1 cup chopped green pepper
4 cloves garlic, minced
1 can (28 oz.) Roma tomatoes,
    undrained and cut up
¼ cup port wine
1 bay leaf
2 teaspoons sugar
½ teaspoon salt
¼ teaspoon saffron threads
    (optional)
⅛ teaspoon pepper
1½ cups water
1½ cups dry white wine
1 tablespoon lemon juice
2 lbs. sunfish, or substitute, fillets
    (2 to 3 oz. each), skin removed

6 servings

In 6-quart Dutch oven or stockpot, heat oil over medium-high heat. Add onions, peppers and garlic. Cook for 3 to 5 minutes, or until vegetables are tender-crisp, stirring constantly.

Stir in tomatoes, port wine, bay leaf, sugar, salt, saffron and pepper. Bring to a boil over medium-high heat. Reduce heat to low. Simmer, uncovered, for 30 minutes. Stir in water, white wine and juice. Cook for 10 to 15 minutes, or until flavors are blended and mixture is hot.

Meanwhile, place sunfish fillets in large skillet. Add just enough water to cover fillets. Bring to a boil over medium-high heat. Reduce heat to low. Simmer for 3 to 4 minutes, or until fish is firm and opaque and just begins to flake. Drain and discard liquid. Add fillets to tomato mixture. Stir gently and cook over low heat until mixture is hot.

Per Serving: Calories: 312 • Protein: 31 g. • Carbohydrate: 13 g. • Fat: 11 g.
• Cholesterol: 101 mg. • Sodium: 525 mg.
Exchanges: 4 lean meat, 1½ vegetable, ½ fruit, ½ fat

South of the Border Cheesy Fish Soup ↑

Merle Ihne – Muscatine, Iowa

½ cup chopped onion
½ cup chopped celery
½ cup chopped red pepper
½ cup chopped green pepper
2 tablespoons margarine or butter
¼ cup all-purpose flour
½ teaspoon salt
⅛ teaspoon pepper
2 cups milk
8 oz. mild Mexican-flavored pasteurized process cheese loaf, cut into 1-inch cubes
1½ cups water
1 teaspoon instant chicken bouillon granules
1½ lbs. yellow perch, or substitute, fillets (2 to 3 oz. each), skin removed, cut into 1-inch pieces
Snipped fresh chives

4 servings

In 6-quart Dutch oven or stockpot, combine onion, celery, peppers and margarine. Cook over medium-high heat for 3 to 4 minutes, or until vegetables are tender, stirring constantly. Reduce heat to medium. Stir in flour, salt and pepper. Blend in milk. Cook over medium heat until mixture thickens and bubbles, stirring constantly. Add cheese. Stir until melted. Remove from heat.

In 2-quart saucepan, combine water and bouillon. Bring to a boil over medium-high heat. Add perch pieces. Return mixture to a boil. Reduce heat to low. Simmer for 8 to 10 minutes, or until fish is firm and opaque and just begins to flake. Add fish and bouillon mixture to cheese mixture. Mix well. Cook over medium heat for 2 to 5 minutes, or until hot, stirring frequently. Sprinkle each serving evenly with chives.

Per Serving: Calories: 486 • Protein: 49 g. • Carbohydrate: 21 g. • Fat: 24 g. • Cholesterol: 210 mg. • Sodium: 1641 mg.
Exchanges: ¼ starch, 6 lean meat, 1 vegetable, ¾ skim milk, 1 fat

Walleye & Clam Chowder ↑

Doris M. Bergquist – Fort Mojave, Arizona

4 slices bacon, cut into 1/2-inch pieces	1/8 teaspoon pepper
1/2 cup thinly sliced celery	3 tablespoons all-purpose flour
1/4 cup sliced green onions	3 cups milk
2 cups peeled cubed red potatoes (3 medium), 1/2-inch cubes	1 1/2 lbs. walleye, or substitute, fillets (6 oz. each), skin removed, cut into 1-inch pieces
1 can (14 1/2 oz.) ready-to-serve chicken broth	1 cup whipping cream
1/2 teaspoon dried dill weed	1 can (6 1/2 oz.) minced clams, undrained
1/2 teaspoon celery seed	1 pkg. (10 oz.) frozen chopped spinach, defrosted and drained
1/4 teaspoon salt	

6 to 8 servings

In 6-quart Dutch oven or stockpot, cook bacon over medium heat until brown and crisp. Drain, reserving 2 tablespoons bacon drippings in Dutch oven. Set bacon aside.

Add celery and onions to bacon drippings in Dutch oven. Cook over medium-high heat for 3 to 5 minutes, or until vegetables are tender-crisp, stirring constantly. Stir in potatoes, broth, dill weed, celery seed, salt and pepper. Bring to a boil over medium-high heat. Reduce heat to low. Simmer, uncovered, for 10 to 15 minutes, or until potatoes are tender.

In 4-cup measure, combine flour and milk. Blend until smooth. Stir into broth mixture. Bring to a boil over medium-high heat. Reduce heat to low. Add walleye pieces. Simmer for 3 minutes, or until fish is firm and opaque and just begins to flake, stirring occasionally. Stir in bacon, cream, clams and spinach. Cook over low heat (do not boil) for 5 minutes, or until chowder is hot, stirring occasionally.

Per Serving: Calories: 355 • Protein: 27 g. • Carbohydrate: 17 g. • Fat: 20 g.
• Cholesterol: 140 mg. • Sodium: 507 mg.
Exchanges: 1/2 starch, 3 lean meat, 1/2 vegetable, 1/2 skim milk, 2 1/4 fat

Fisherman's Chowder

"This is an original recipe, often altered by available ingredients and the mood of the moment, but always a crowd-pleaser."
Marla Hart Clark – Moriarty, New Mexico

1 1/2 lbs. yellow perch, bass, or substitute, fillets (3 to 6 oz. each), skin removed, cut into 1-inch pieces
1/4 cup all-purpose flour
2 tablespoons margarine or butter
2 cans (10 3/4 oz. each) condensed cream of mushroom soup
2 cups milk
2 cups peeled cubed red potatoes (3 medium), 1/2-inch cubes
1 cup chopped carrots
1 can (6 oz.) lump crabmeat, rinsed, drained and cartilage removed
1/2 cup chopped celery
1 tablespoon dried parsley flakes
1/2 teaspoon dried dill weed
1/2 teaspoon garlic powder
1/4 teaspoon pepper

6 servings

In shallow mixing bowl, combine perch pieces and flour. Toss gently to coat. In 6-quart Dutch oven or stockpot, melt margarine over medium-high heat. Add fish. Cook for 3 to 5 minutes, or until lightly browned, stirring constantly.

Add remaining ingredients. Bring to a boil over medium-high heat. Reduce heat to low. Simmer, uncovered, for 30 to 40 minutes, or until fish is firm and opaque and just begins to flake, stirring occasionally.

Per Serving: Calories: 391 • Protein: 34 g.
• Carbohydrate: 27 g. • Fat: 16 g.
• Cholesterol: 140 mg. • Sodium: 1101 mg.
Exchanges: 1 1/2 starch, 4 lean meat, 1 vegetable, 3/4 fat

Picante Fish Chowder

Vicki J. Snyder – Columbus, Ohio

2 slices bacon, cut into ½-inch pieces
1 cup peeled cubed red potatoes, ½-inch cubes
½ cup chopped onion
½ cup chopped carrot
½ cup finely chopped zucchini
½ cup chopped celery
½ cup frozen corn
1½ lbs. yellow perch, bass, or substitute, fillets (3 to 6 oz. each), skin removed, cut into 1-inch pieces
2 cups water
1 can (14½ oz.) whole tomatoes, undrained and cut up
½ cup picante sauce
1 tablespoon Worcestershire sauce
¼ teaspoon salt
¼ teaspoon pepper
Snipped fresh parsley

6 servings

In 6-quart Dutch oven or stockpot, cook bacon over medium heat until brown and crisp. Add potatoes, onion, carrot, zucchini, celery and corn. Cook over medium-high heat for 3 to 5 minutes, or until vegetables are tender-crisp, stirring constantly.

Add remaining ingredients, except parsley. Bring to a boil over medium-high heat. Reduce heat to low. Simmer, uncovered, for 30 to 45 minutes, or until potatoes are tender, stirring occasionally. Sprinkle each serving evenly with parsley.

Per Serving: Calories: 238 • Protein: 24 g. • Carbohydrate: 15 g.
• Fat: 9 g. • Cholesterol: 82 mg. • Sodium: 504 mg.
Exchanges: ½ starch, 3 lean meat, 1½ vegetable

Salmon Chowder

"The trick is to cook fish and potatoes separately. The final result is a smooth chowder."
Gary Livingston – Middleburg Heights, Ohio

2-lb. salmon, or substitute, fillet,
    skin on
1 recipe Court Bouillon, page 42
2 cups peeled cubed red potatoes
    (3 medium), ½-inch cubes
8 slices bacon
2 cups chopped onions
8 oz. fresh mushrooms, sliced
    (2 cups)
1 cup chopped celery
1 cup water
½ teaspoon salt
¼ teaspoon pepper
1 quart half-and-half

6 servings

Poach salmon in Court Bouillon as directed. Drain and discard poaching liquid. Cool fish slightly. Remove skin and bones; flake meat. Set aside.

Place potatoes in 2-quart saucepan. Add just enough water to cover potatoes. Bring to a boil over medium-high heat. Reduce heat to low. Simmer for 5 to 10 minutes, or until potatoes are tender. Drain. Set aside.

In 6-quart Dutch oven or stockpot, cook bacon over medium heat until brown and crisp. Drain, reserving 2 tablespoons bacon drippings in Dutch oven. Crumble bacon and add back to bacon drippings. Add onions, mushrooms, celery, 1 cup water, the salt and pepper. Bring to a boil over medium-high heat. Reduce heat to low. Simmer for 6 to 8 minutes, or until vegetables are tender, stirring once or twice.

Stir in fish, potatoes and half-and-half. Cook over low heat (do not boil) for 10 to 15 minutes, or until hot, stirring occasionally. Sprinkle each serving evenly with snipped fresh parsley, if desired.

Per Serving: Calories: 573 • Protein: 40 g. • Carbohydrate: 22 g. • Fat: 36 g.
• Cholesterol: 153 mg. • Sodium: 494 mg.
Exchanges: ½ starch, 5 lean meat, 1 vegetable, ½ skim milk, 4 fat

Dixie Panfish Chowder

"This was my grandmother's recipe. My mother use to make this for us on our streamside cook-outs."
    Keith Sutton – Benton, Arkansas

    4 slices bacon
    ½ cup chopped onion
    ½ cup chopped carrot
    ¼ cup chopped celery
    1 lb. yellow perch, or substitute,
         fillets (2 to 3 oz. each), skin
         removed, cut into 1-inch
         pieces
    1 can (16 oz.) whole Irish potatoes,
         rinsed, drained and cut into
         ½-inch cubes
    1 cup water
    ½ teaspoon salt
    ¼ teaspoon pepper
    1 cup milk
    1 can (16½ oz.) cream-style corn

                                    4 servings

In 6-quart Dutch oven or stockpot, cook bacon over medium heat until brown and crisp. Drain, reserving 2 tablespoons bacon drippings in Dutch oven. Crumble bacon. Set aside.

Add onion, carrot and celery to bacon drippings in Dutch oven. Cook over medium-high heat for 3 to 5 minutes, or until vegetables are tender-crisp, stirring constantly. Stir in perch pieces, potatoes, water, salt and pepper. Bring to a boil over medium-high heat. Reduce heat to low. Simmer, covered, for 8 to 10 minutes, or until fish is firm and opaque and just begins to flake.

Blend in milk and corn. Cook over medium heat (do not boil) for 5 to 7 minutes, or until mixture is hot, stirring occasionally. Sprinkle each serving evenly with crumbled bacon.

Per Serving: Calories: 368 • Protein: 29 g. • Carbohydrate: 38 g. • Fat: 12 g. • Cholesterol: 121 mg. • Sodium: 852 mg. Exchanges: 1¾ starch, 3 lean meat, ½ vegetable, ¼ skim milk, ¾ fat

Clif's Hearty Fish Chowder ↑

"We prefer lake trout or salmon, but any kind of fish can be used."
    Clif and Betty Santa – Vermilion Bay, Ontario

    4 cups peeled cubed red potatoes
         (6 medium), ½-inch cubes
    2 teaspoons salt
    15 whole peppercorns
    6 whole allspice
    ½ cup margarine or butter
    1 can (12 oz.) evaporated milk

    2 medium onions, thinly sliced
    2 lbs. any freshwater fish fillets
         (8 oz. each), skin removed,
         cut into 2-inch pieces
    3 tablespoons snipped fresh
         parsley

                                    8 servings

Place potatoes in 4-quart Dutch oven or stockpot. Add just enough water to cover potatoes. Bring to a boil over medium-high heat. Add salt, peppercorns and allspice. Cook for 3 to 5 minutes, or until potatoes are tender-crisp. Reduce heat to medium-low. Add margarine and milk. Stir until margarine is melted.

Layer onion slices over potatoes. Arrange salmon pieces on top of onions. Simmer (do not boil) for 20 to 30 minutes, or until fish is firm and opaque and just begins to flake and onions are tender, turning salmon pieces over once or twice. Sprinkle each serving evenly with parsley.

Per Serving: Calories: 401 • Protein: 29 g. • Carbohydrate: 20 g. • Fat: 23 g. • Cholesterol: 80 mg. • Sodium: 800 mg. Exchanges: 1 starch, 3 lean meat, ⅓ skim milk, 2¾ fat

Hearty Catfish Stew

Thomas K. Squier –
Aberdeen, North Carolina

2 cups peeled cubed red potatoes
(3 medium), ½-inch cubes
2 cups seeded chopped tomatoes
1 cup chopped onions
1 cup chopped green pepper
1 cup frozen corn
1 cup tomato juice
1 cup water
2 tablespoons margarine or butter
2 cloves garlic, minced
½ teaspoon salt
½ teaspoon dried thyme leaves
(optional)
¼ teaspoon pepper
⅛ to ¼ teaspoon cayenne
4 catfish fillets (6 oz. each), skin
removed, cut into 1-inch pieces

4 servings

In 6-quart Dutch oven or stockpot,
combine all ingredients, except catfish pieces. Bring to a boil over
medium-high heat. Reduce heat
to low. Simmer, uncovered, for 10
to 12 minutes, or until potatoes
are tender, stirring occasionally.

Add catfish. Simmer for 10 to 15
minutes, or until fish is firm and
opaque and just begins to flake,
stirring occasionally.

Per Serving: Calories: 395 • Protein: 36 g.
• Carbohydrate: 33 g. • Fat: 14 g.
• Cholesterol: 99 mg. • Sodium: 684 mg.
Exchanges: 1¼ starch, 4 lean meat,
2 vegetable, ¼ fat

Snapping Turtle Stew

Thomas K. Squier – Aberdeen, North Carolina

  2 lbs. snapping turtle meat, trimmed and cut into
      1-inch cubes
  4 cups seeded chopped tomatoes
4¼ cups water, divided
  1 cup chopped onions
  ½ teaspoon salt
  ½ teaspoon dried thyme leaves
  ¼ teaspoon dried rosemary leaves
  ¼ teaspoon pepper
  ¼ teaspoon ground nutmeg
  ⅛ teaspoon ground cloves
  1 tablespoon lemon juice
  2 tablespoons all-purpose flour
  ½ cup snipped fresh parsley
  ¼ cup dry sherry

In 6-quart Dutch oven or stockpot, combine turtle meat, tomatoes, 4 cups water, the onions, salt, thyme, rosemary, pepper, nutmeg, cloves and juice. Bring to a boil over medium-high heat, stirring occasionally. Reduce heat to low. Simmer, uncovered, for 2¼ to 2½ hours, or until meat is tender, stirring occasionally.

In small bowl, combine flour and remaining ¼ cup water. Blend until smooth. Add to stew, stirring constantly, until mixture thickens and bubbles. Just before serving, stir in parsley and sherry.

Nutritional information not available.

4 servings

UTENSILS for oven cooking include (1) broiling pan with rack; (2) baking pan or roaster with 2-inch sides for oven frying; (3) large spatula, for handling whole fish; (4) glass baking dishes; (5) deep-dish pie plate; (6) baster; (7) casserole; (8) porcelain enamel or (9) teflon-coated baking pans and (10) heavy-duty foil.

Techniques for Oven Cooking

The three basic methods for oven cooking fish are baking, broiling and oven frying. Any fish can be cooked in an oven, but some of these methods work better than others for specific kinds and cuts of fish.

BAKING. This technique is used most often for oily fish because they're not likely to dry out. But lean fish can also be baked if you marinate them first, coat them with crumbs or sauce or bake them in a small amount of liquid, which is then used for basting.

Other ways to conserve moisture are to bake the fish in a covered pan or wrap it with aluminum foil, vegetable leaves or oiled baking paper. These techniques also help retain flavor.

You can bake steaks, fillets or whole fish. The latter are often stuffed to add flavor and keep them moist. The baking temperature and time depend on the thickness. Fish more than 3 inches thick are usually baked at 325 to 375°F; fish less than 1 inch, 400 to 450°F. As a rule, bake 10 minutes per inch of thickness.

BROILING. This high-heat cooking technique browns the fish more than baking does, adding extra flavor. The fish are placed on a broiler pan that has been sprayed with nonstick vegetable cooking spray or brushed with vegetable oil. Adjust the oven rack so that the surface of the fish is 4 to 6 inches below the broiling element; cook for approximately 6 to 8 minutes per inch of thickness (slightly less under a gas broiler). If the fish are more than ¾ inch thick, they should be turned over after about half the cooking time and broiled on the other side or cooked at a greater distance from the broiling element.

Broiling is an excellent way to cook fatty fish, such as lake trout, because much of the fat drains into the broiler pan. You can also broil lean fish, but they may dry out unless you keep them farther from the heating element and baste them periodically with butter, margarine, vegetable oil or a marinade.

The technique works best with steaks or fillets, but whole fish can also be broiled if you slash the sides as shown at right. Because of the intense heat, you must watch the fish closely as it broils, lowering the oven rack, if necessary, so the outside doesn't overcook before the inside is done.

OVEN FRYING. With this technique, you get the flavor and crispness of panfried fish without a lot of fuss. Just leave them in the pan until they're done. Oven frying works best with fillets.

The fish is prepared the same way as for panfrying. Dip it first in an egg and milk mixture, then dredge it in flour, cornmeal or any seasoned coating mix.

Place the prepared fish in a heated pan with ⅛ inch of vegetable oil. Turn the fish over to coat both sides with oil. Cook in the oven without turning for 10 minutes per inch of thickness.

BROWN baked steaks or fillets by basting them with pan juices and then placing them under the broiler for one or two minutes.

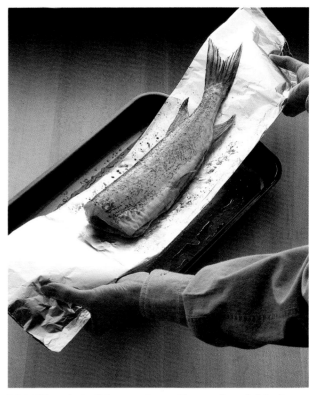

PLACE a whole fish on a piece of heavy-duty foil before baking. Remove from oven; cool slightly. This way you can pick up the foil and remove the cooked fish in one piece.

POUR ¼ to ½ inch liquid, such as fish stock, wine, beer or vegetable juice, into the broiler pan before broiling. This adds moisture and flavor during cooking.

SLASH whole fish on both sides before broiling. Cuts about ¼ to ½ inch deep ensure that the fish will cook through evenly.

← Stuffed Brookies

"Works best with freshly caught trout. Serve with a white zinfandel."
Bernard T. Nowacki – Rio Rico, Arizona

¼ cup margarine or butter, divided
¼ cup chopped onion
¼ cup chopped red pepper
¼ cup chopped green pepper
8 to 10 slices day-old French bread, ¼ inch thick, cut into ¼-inch cubes (1½ cups)
1 can (4½ oz.) small deveined shrimp, rinsed, drained and chopped
¼ cup clam juice
1 egg
1 tablespoon snipped fresh cilantro leaves
¼ teaspoon salt
⅛ teaspoon cayenne
4 whole drawn stream trout (8 oz. each), heads removed
⅛ teaspoon pepper

4 servings

Heat oven to 375°F. In 10-inch skillet, melt 2 tablespoons margarine over medium heat. Add chopped onion and peppers. Cook for 3 to 4 minutes, or until tender-crisp. Remove from heat. In medium mixing bowl, combine onion mixture and remaining ingredients, except trout and pepper. Set aside.

In 1-quart saucepan, melt remaining 2 tablespoons margarine over medium heat. Brush exterior and cavity of each fish with half of margarine. Sprinkle cavities evenly with pepper.

Spray 8-inch square baking dish with nonstick vegetable cooking spray. Arrange trout cavity-sides-up in prepared dish. (Use crushed pieces of foil between fish as necessary to keep fish propped upright.) Stuff each fish evenly with stuffing mixture. Drizzle with reserved margarine. Bake for 15 to 20 minutes, or until fish is firm and opaque and just begins to flake.

Per Serving: Calories: 369 • Protein: 38 g. • Carbohydrate: 10 g. • Fat: 19 g. • Cholesterol: 185 mg. • Sodium: 495 mg.
Exchanges: ½ starch, 5 lean meat, ½ vegetable, 1 fat

Trout Baked in Wine →

Peter R. Lebengood – Wyomissing, Pennsylvania

6 whole drawn stream trout (8 oz. each)
2 tablespoons fresh lemon juice
½ teaspoon salt
½ teaspoon pepper
½ cup thinly sliced green onions
2 tablespoons snipped fresh parsley
1 cup Chablis or other dry white wine

6 servings

Heat oven to 400°F. Spray 13 × 9-inch baking dish with nonstick vegetable cooking spray. Set aside. Brush cavity of each trout evenly with juice. Sprinkle cavities evenly with salt and pepper.

Arrange fish in single layer in prepared dish. Sprinkle with onions and parsley. Pour wine evenly over fish. Bake for 25 to 30 minutes, or until fish begins to flake when fork is inserted at backbone in thickest part of fish, basting once or twice. Garnish with additional fresh parsley sprigs and lemon slices, if desired.

Per Serving: Calories: 165 • Protein: 28 g. • Carbohydrate: 1 g. • Fat: 5 g. • Cholesterol: 76 mg. • Sodium: 221 mg.
Exchanges: 3 lean meat

Baked Trout Vermilion

Jude W. Theriot – Lake Charles, Louisianna

1 whole drawn lake trout or
   substitute (8½ lbs.), head
   and tail removed
2 tablespoons margarine or butter
1 cup chopped onions
¼ green pepper, cut into thin strips
1 large clove garlic, minced
8 oz. fresh mushrooms, thinly
   sliced (2 cups)
2 tablespoons fresh lemon juice
¼ teaspoon red pepper sauce

10 servings

Heat oven to 325°F. Butterfly trout
as shown below.

Place fish skin-side-down on
15½ × 10½ × 1-inch jelly roll
pan. Dot evenly with margarine.
In medium mixing bowl, combine
onions, pepper strips and garlic.
Sprinkle mixture evenly over fish.
Cover with foil. Bake for 45 minutes. Remove foil. Sprinkle mushrooms evenly over fish. Re-cover.
Bake for 15 to 20 minutes, or until
fish is firm and opaque and just
begins to flake.

In small bowl, combine juice and red
pepper sauce. Before serving,
sprinkle evenly over fish.

Per Serving: Calories: 332 • Protein: 42 g.
• Carbohydrate: 3 g. • Fat: 16 g.
• Cholesterol: 117 mg. • Sodium: 136 mg.
Exchanges: 6 lean meat, ½ vegetable

How to Butterfly Whole Fish

CUT from inside cavity along each side of backbone to
release bone from flesh; do not cut through skin.

DISCARD bone and spread out two sides of fish so it lies
flat. Trim and discard belly meat. Remove rib bones.

74

Baked Alaskan Salmon, Homesteader-style ↑

"This recipe belonged to an old homesteader living in Alaska. The red pepper sauce gives a unique mouth-watering flavor that is almost Cajun."
    Steven F. Gruber – Bemidji, Minnesota

     1   whole drawn salmon or substitute (2¾ lbs.), head removed
    ½   teaspoon salt
    ¼   teaspoon pepper
    1½ cups reduced-calorie mayonnaise
     1   cup finely chopped onions
    ½   cup finely chopped green pepper
    ½   cup finely chopped red pepper
    ⅓   cup packed brown sugar
    ⅓   cup pickle relish
    ⅓   cup lemon juice
     1   teaspoon red pepper sauce

                                                    6 servings

Heat oven to 325°F. Sprinkle cavity of fish evenly with salt and pepper. Cut 20 × 18-inch sheet of heavy-duty foil. Place in 13 × 9-inch baking dish, with ends hanging over. Place salmon in dish. Set aside.

In medium mixing bowl, combine remaining ingredients. Spoon some of mixture into cavity of fish. Spoon remaining mixture evenly over fish. Fold long sides of foil together in locked folds. Fold and crimp short ends; seal tightly. Bake for 1 hour to 1 hour 15 minutes, or until fish begins to flake when fork is inserted at backbone in thickest part of fish.

Per Serving: Calories: 385 • Protein: 26 g. • Carbohydrate: 24 g. • Fat: 21 g. • Cholesterol: 84 mg. • Sodium: 714 mg. Exchanges: 3½ lean meat, 1 vegetable, 1¼ fruit, 2 fat

Baked Stuffed Trout

    Mary B. Starinovich – Stafford Springs, Connecticut

    ¼   cup margarine or butter
     1   small onion, chopped (¾ cup)
     1   stalk celery, chopped (½ cup)
     2   slices bread, cut into ¼-inch cubes (1½ cups)
     1   jar (4½ oz.) sliced mushrooms, drained
     1   dill pickle spear, finely chopped (¼ cup)
     1   tablespoon lemon juice
     1   teaspoon dried parsley flakes
    ½   teaspoon salt
    ¼   teaspoon dried basil leaves
    ⅛   teaspoon garlic powder
     2   tablespoons vegetable oil
     4   whole drawn stream trout (8 oz. each)

                                                    4 servings

Heat oven to 350°F. In 10-inch skillet, melt margarine over medium heat. Add onion and celery. Cook for 3 to 5 minutes, or until tender. Remove from heat. Stir in remaining ingredients, except oil and trout. Set aside.

Pour oil into 13 × 9-inch baking dish. Roll each trout in oil to coat. Stuff each trout evenly with stuffing mixture. Arrange trout in single layer in prepared dish, spreading any additional stuffing mixture between trout. Bake for 25 to 30 minutes, or until fish begins to flake when fork is inserted at backbone in thickest part of fish.

Per Serving: Calories: 374 • Protein: 30 g. • Carbohydrate: 11 g. • Fat: 23 g. • Cholesterol: 77 mg. • Sodium: 796 mg. Exchanges: ½ starch, 4 lean meat, ½ vegetable, 2¼ fat

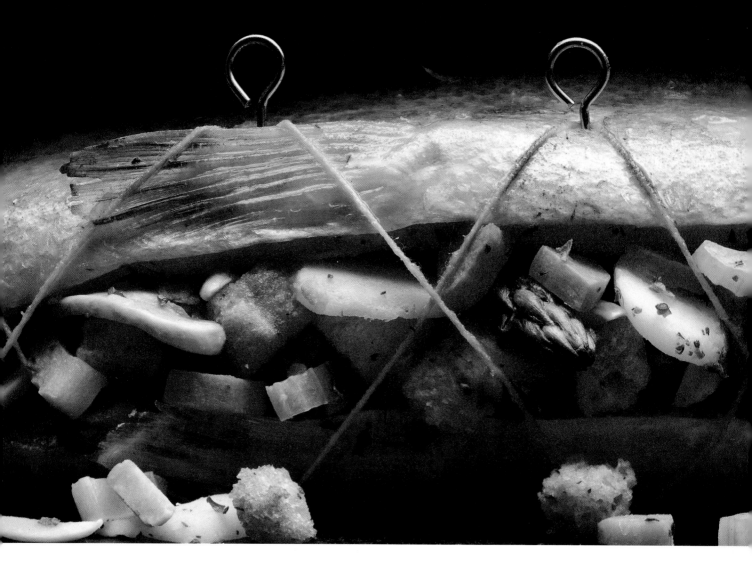

Trout Valora ↑

"Valora is a small town in northwestern Ontario near several lakes with great lake-trout fishing."
  Bill Diedrich – Minnetonka, Minnesota

⅓ cup margarine or butter
 1 cup chopped onions
 1 cup chopped celery
 1 cup chopped carrots
 4 oz. fresh mushrooms, sliced (1 cup)
½ cup chopped fresh asparagus spears
 1 can (8 oz.) sliced water chestnuts, rinsed and
     drained
 2 cups unseasoned dry bread cubes
¼ cup plus 2 tablespoons toasted slivered almonds
¼ cup half-and-half
 2 tablespoons snipped fresh parsley
 1 teaspoon bouquet garni seasoning
½ teaspoon salt
 1 whole drawn lake trout or substitute (6½ to
     8½ lbs.), head and tail removed

BASTING SAUCE:

⅓ cup margarine or butter, melted
 1 teaspoon grated lemon peel
¼ cup plus 2 tablespoons lemon juice

8 to 10 servings

Heat oven to 375°F. In 12-inch skillet, melt ⅓ cup margarine over medium-low heat. Add onions, celery, carrots, mushrooms, asparagus and water chestnuts. Cook for 8 to 10 minutes, or until vegetables are tender, stirring frequently. Remove from heat.

In large mixing bowl, combine vegetable mixture, bread cubes, almonds, half-and-half, parsley, bouquet garni and salt. Spoon stuffing mixture into cavity of trout. Wrap any extra stuffing in foil packet. Set aside. Insert short metal skewers through underbelly of fish, and lace cavity shut by crisscrossing with string.

In 1-cup measure, combine basting sauce ingredients. Set aside. Spray 15½ × 10½ × 1-inch jelly roll pan with nonstick vegetable cooking spray. Place fish and stuffing packet on prepared pan. Bake for 1 hour to 1 hour 10 minutes, or until fish begins to flake when fork is inserted at backbone in thickest part of fish, basting frequently with sauce during baking.

Per Serving: Calories: 490 • Protein: 45 g. • Carbohydrate: 11 g. • Fat: 29 g. • Cholesterol: 119 mg. • Sodium: 408 mg.
Exchanges: ½ starch, 6 lean meat, 1 vegetable, 2 fat

Italian Cheese & Spinach Stuffed Trout

Al Weber – Glendale, New York

¼ cup olive oil, divided
½ cup finely chopped onion
3 cloves garlic, minced
1½ cups torn fresh spinach leaves
¾ cup unseasoned dry bread
 crumbs
¼ cup shredded fresh Parmesan
 cheese
3 tablespoons snipped fresh parsley
1 tablespoon fresh lemon juice
½ teaspoon Italian seasoning
¼ teaspoon freshly ground pepper
¼ teaspoon salt
4 whole drawn stream trout
 (8 oz. each)
⅓ cup dry white wine

4 servings

Heat oven to 350°F. In 10-inch skillet, heat 2 tablespoons oil over medium heat. Add onion and garlic. Cook for 3 to 4 minutes, or until onion is tender. Stir in spinach. Cook just until spinach is wilted. Remove from heat. Stir in bread crumbs, Parmesan cheese, parsley, juice and seasonings. Set stuffing mixture aside.

Pour remaining 2 tablespoons oil into 13 × 9-inch baking dish. Roll each trout in oil to coat. Stuff each trout evenly with stuffing mixture. Arrange trout in single layer in prepared dish, spreading any additional stuffing mixture between trout. Pour wine evenly over fish. Bake for 25 to 30 minutes, or until fish begins to flake when fork is inserted at backbone in thickest part of fish.

Per Serving: Calories: 397 • Protein: 33 g. • Carbohydrate: 18 g. • Fat: 21 g.
• Cholesterol: 82 mg. • Sodium: 444 mg.
Exchanges: 1 starch, 4 lean meat, ½ vegetable, 2 fat

Rosemary Trout al Cartoccio

"Cartoccio is Italian for paper bag."
  Richard J. Parmley – St. Louis, Missouri

  6 whole drawn stream trout (8 oz. each)
 ½ teaspoon salt
 ½ teaspoon pepper
  6 sprigs fresh rosemary (2 inches long)
 ⅓ cup olive oil

6 servings

Per Serving: Calories: 219 • Protein: 28 g. • Carbohydrate: 0
• Fat: 11 g. • Cholesterol: 76 mg. • Sodium: 219 mg.
Exchanges: 4 lean meat

78

How to Make Rosemary Trout al Cartoccio

POSITION oven rack in center of oven. Heat to 400°F. Cut
six 16 × 10-inch sheets of brown paper from grocery bags.
(Do not use imprinted bags or glued sides of bags.)

SPRINKLE cavity of each trout evenly with salt and pepper. Place 1 sprig of rosemary in each cavity. Set aside.

BRUSH one side of 1 sheet of paper generously with oil
until nearly transparent. Top with second sheet of paper.
Repeat brushing. Repeat with remaining sheets of paper.

PLACE 1 trout in center of each sheet of paper. Roll up
each trout in paper, twisting ends to seal. Place packets
directly on center oven rack, spacing at least 1 inch apart.

BAKE for 15 to 20 minutes, or until fish begins to flake
when fork is inserted at backbone in thickest part of fish.
Using scissors, cut packets down center to open. Squeeze
fresh lemon juice over trout, if desired.

Salmon with Tarragon Sauce →

George Gruenefeld – Montreal, Quebec

1 whole drawn salmon or
  substitute (3½ to 4½ lbs.),
  head removed
2 tablespoons snipped fresh
  parsley or 1 teaspoon dried
  parsley flakes
1 tablespoon snipped fresh
  tarragon leaves or ½ teaspoon
  dried tarragon leaves
¼ teaspoon salt
¼ teaspoon paprika
⅛ teaspoon pepper
1 tablespoon fresh lemon juice

SAUCE:
¼ cup margarine or butter
¼ cup all-purpose flour
1 tablespoon snipped fresh
  tarragon leaves or ½ teaspoon
  dried tarragon leaves
½ teaspoon curry powder
¼ teaspoon salt
⅛ teaspoon pepper
1 cup ready-to-serve chicken broth
1 cup milk
2 tablespoons dry white wine

6 to 8 servings

Heat oven to 375°F. Cut 28 × 18-inch sheet of heavy-duty foil. Place salmon on foil. Sprinkle cavity and outside of fish with parsley, 1 tablespoon tarragon, ¼ teaspoon salt and paprika, ⅛ teaspoon pepper and the juice. Fold long sides of foil together in locked folds. Fold and crimp short ends; seal tightly. Place on large baking sheet. Bake for 40 to 50 minutes, or until fish begins to flake when fork is inserted at backbone in thickest part of fish.

Meanwhile, prepare sauce. In 2-quart saucepan, melt margarine over medium heat. Stir in flour, tarragon, curry, salt and pepper. Blend in broth and milk. Cook over medium heat for 3 to 5 minutes, or until mixture thickens and bubbles, stirring constantly. Stir in wine. Serve salmon with sauce. Garnish with additional fresh tarragon sprigs, if desired.

Per Serving: Calories: 233 • Protein: 22 g.
• Carbohydrate: 5 g. • Fat: 13 g.
• Cholesterol: 59 mg. • Sodium: 385 mg.
Exchanges: ⅓ starch, 3 lean meat, 1 fat

Wine-baked Salmon Steaks

Vicki J. Snyder – Columbus, Ohio

1 tablespoon margarine or butter,
  divided
4 salmon, or substitute, steaks
  (8 oz. each), 1 inch thick
1 tablespoon lemon juice
½ teaspoon salt
¼ teaspoon pepper
¼ teaspoon dried oregano leaves
¼ teaspoon garlic powder
¼ teaspoon crushed red pepper
  flakes
½ cup dry white wine

4 servings

Heat oven to 375°F. Lightly grease 13 × 9-inch baking dish with 1 teaspoon margarine. Arrange salmon steaks in single layer in prepared dish. Dot with remaining 2 teaspoons margarine. Sprinkle steaks evenly with juice, salt, pepper, oregano, garlic powder and red pepper flakes. Pour wine around steaks into dish. Bake, uncovered, for 15 to 20 minutes, or until fish is firm and opaque and just begins to flake, basting twice.

Per Serving: Calories: 331 • Protein: 40 g. • Carbohydrate: 1 g. • Fat: 16 g.
• Cholesterol: 110 mg. • Sodium: 397 mg.
Exchanges: 6 lean meat

Marinated Salmon Steaks

Vicki J. Snyder – Columbus, Ohio

MARINADE:

- 1 tablespoon grated orange peel
- ½ cup orange juice
- 1 tablespoon lemon juice
- 1 clove garlic, minced
- ½ teaspoon dried parsley flakes
- ¼ teaspoon dried tarragon leaves

- 4 salmon, or substitute, steaks (8 oz. each), 1 inch thick
- 2 tablespoons margarine or butter, melted

4 servings

In large plastic food-storage bag, combine marinade ingredients. Add salmon steaks. Secure bag. Turn to coat. Chill 1 to 2 hours, turning bag occasionally.

Spray rack in broiler pan with non-stick vegetable cooking spray. Drain and discard marinade from steaks. Arrange steaks on prepared broiler pan. Brush evenly with melted margarine. Place under broiler with surface of fish 6 inches from heat. Broil for 5 minutes. Turn steaks over. Broil for 8 to 10 minutes longer, or until fish is firm and opaque and just begins to flake.

Per Serving: Calories: 345 • Protein: 40 g.
• Carbohydrate: 2 g. • Fat: 19 g.
• Cholesterol: 110 mg. • Sodium: 155 mg.
Exchanges: 6 lean meat

Carrot-topped Baked Fish ↑

Ronald E. Fredrick – Algonquin, Illinois

- 1½ lbs. any freshwater fish fillets (6 oz. each), skin removed
- 2 cups grated carrots
- 3 tablespoons margarine or butter, melted
- 2 tablespoons lemon juice
- ¼ teaspoon ground thyme
- ¼ teaspoon salt
- 3 tablespoons margarine or butter
- 3 tablespoons plus 1½ teaspoons all-purpose flour
- ¼ teaspoon salt
- ¼ teaspoon pepper
- ⅓ cup milk

4 servings

Heat oven to 450°F. Spray 13 × 9-inch baking dish with nonstick vegetable cooking spray. Arrange fillets, slightly overlapping, in prepared dish. Set aside.

In medium mixing bowl, combine carrots, melted margarine, juice, thyme and salt. Spread mixture evenly over fillets. Cover with foil. Bake for 25 to 35 minutes, or until fish is firm and opaque and just begins to flake. Drain liquid from fish into 2-cup measure. Cover fish with foil to keep warm. Set aside.

Add water to liquid in cup to equal 1⅓ cups. In 1-quart saucepan, melt 3 tablespoons margarine over medium heat. Stir in flour, salt and pepper. Blend in cooking liquid mixture and milk. Cook for 5 to 7 minutes, or until mixture thickens and bubbles, stirring constantly. Pour sauce evenly over fish. Garnish with sliced green onions and lemon slices, and serve over rice, if desired.

Per Serving: Calories: 376 • Protein: 35 g. • Carbohydrate: 13 g. • Fat: 20 g.
• Cholesterol: 149 mg. • Sodium: 588 mg.
Exchanges: ½ starch, 4½ lean meat, 1 vegetable, 1¼ fat

Zesty Baked Walleye Supreme

Jim Roth – Alvordton, Ohio

2¼ lbs. walleye, or substitute, fillets (6 oz. each), skin removed
3 tablespoons margarine or butter
3 tablespoons lemon juice
1 teaspoon red pepper sauce
½ teaspoon Worcestershire sauce
½ teaspoon salt
⅛ to ¼ teaspoon cayenne
½ cup thinly sliced celery
1 medium red onion, thinly sliced, separated into rings
¼ cup diagonally sliced green onions
½ medium green pepper, thinly sliced
½ medium red pepper, thinly sliced

6 servings

Position oven rack in center of oven. Heat oven to 350°F. Spray 13 × 9-inch baking dish with nonstick vegetable cooking spray. Arrange fillets, slightly overlapping, in prepared dish. Set aside.

In 1-quart saucepan, melt margarine over medium heat. Remove from heat. Add juice, red pepper sauce, Worcestershire sauce, salt and cayenne. Baste fillets with half of margarine mixture. Layer celery, onion and pepper slices evenly over fillets. Drizzle remaining margarine mixture over fish. Cover dish with foil.

Bake for 35 to 40 minutes, or until fish is firm and opaque and just begins to flake. Remove foil. Broil for 8 to 10 minutes, or until peppers and onions are lightly browned. Lift out whole fillets with vegetables and place on serving platter.

Per Serving: Calories: 222 • Protein: 33 g. • Carbohydrate: 3 g. • Fat: 8 g.
• Cholesterol: 146 mg. • Sodium: 374 mg.
Exchanges: 4 lean meat, 1 vegetable

Yellow Perch Baked in Apples & Mustard

Annette Bignami – Moscow, Idaho

¼ cup plus 2 tablespoons
    margarine or butter, divided
3 medium red cooking apples
    (8 oz. each), cored and cut
    into ¼-inch slices
1½ lbs. yellow perch, or substitute,
    fillets (2 to 3 oz. each), skin
    removed
⅓ cup Dijon mustard
1 teaspoon sugar
2 cups white wine, divided
1 cup clam juice
1 tablespoon sliced green onion

4 servings

Heat oven to 350°F. In 12-inch skillet, melt 3 tablespoons margarine over medium heat. Add apple slices. Cook for 6 to 8 minutes, or until lightly browned, stirring frequently. Remove from heat. Set aside.

Spray 13 × 9-inch baking dish with nonstick vegetable cooking spray. Arrange fillets, slightly overlapping, in prepared dish. Spread mustard evenly over fillets. Sprinkle with sugar. Layer apple slices over and around fillets. Set skillet aside. Pour 1 cup wine and the clam juice over fillets. Bake for 15 to 20 minutes, or until fish is firm and opaque and just begins to flake. Drain and reserve liquid from baking dish. Cover fish to keep warm. Set aside.

Meanwhile, in same skillet, combine remaining 1 cup wine and the onion. Simmer over medium heat until liquid is reduced to 1 tablespoon. Remove from heat. Add reserved liquid to reduced liquid in skillet. Simmer mixture over medium heat until reduced by half. Add remaining 3 tablespoons margarine to reduced mixture. Cook for 1 to 2 minutes, or until sauce is glossy and slightly thickened, stirring constantly. Pour sauce over fillets and apples. Serve with hot cooked rice or egg noodles, if desired.

Per Serving: Calories: 435 • Protein: 34 g. • Carbohydrate: 29 g. • Fat: 21 g.
• Cholesterol: 153 mg. • Sodium: 1035 mg.
Exchanges: 4½ lean meat, 2 fruit, 1½ fat

Cheesy Baked Catfish →

"I like to serve this with a tossed salad."
Virgil R. Meyer – Laverne, Oklahoma

    1   cup crushed cheese-flavored
            crackers
    ¼   cup sesame seed
    1   tablespoon snipped fresh parsley
    ½   teaspoon salt
    ¼   teaspoon pepper
    ¼   teaspoon cayenne
    ½   cup margarine or butter
    2¼ lbs. catfish fillets (6 oz. each),
            skin removed
    2   tablespoons shredded fresh
            Parmesan cheese

                                6 servings

Heat oven to 400°F. In shallow dish, combine crackers, sesame seed, parsley, salt, pepper and cayenne. Set aside.

In 1-quart saucepan, melt margarine over medium heat. Pour into another shallow dish. Dip each fillet first in margarine and then in crumb mixture, pressing lightly to coat.

Arrange fillets in single layer in 13 × 9-inch baking dish. Bake for 20 to 25 minutes, or until fish is firm and opaque and just begins to flake. Sprinkle fillets evenly with Parmesan cheese.

Per Serving: Calories: 447 • Protein: 34 g. • Carbohydrate: 10 g. • Fat: 30 g. • Cholesterol: 100 mg. • Sodium: 707 mg. Exchanges: ¾ starch, 4½ lean meat, 3¼ fat

Baked Bass Italienne

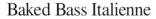

Thomas K. Squier – Aberdeen, North Carolina

    1   tablespoon olive oil
    2   cups finely chopped onions
    3   large tomatoes, peeled, seeded
            and chopped (3 cups)
    1   teaspoon Italian seasoning
    ½   teaspoon salt
    ¼   teaspoon pepper
    2¼ lbs. bass, or substitute, fillets
            (6 oz. each), skin removed
    ¼   cup sliced pimiento-stuffed
            olives

                                6 servings

Heat oven to 375°F. In 12-inch skillet, heat oil over medium-low heat. Add onions. Cook for 4 to 5 minutes, or until onions are tender-crisp, stirring frequently. Stir in tomatoes and seasonings. Increase heat to medium. Simmer mixture for 8 to 10 minutes, or until liquid evaporates, stirring frequently. Remove from heat. Set aside.

Spray 13 × 9-inch baking dish with nonstick vegetable cooking spray. Spread tomato mixture evenly in prepared dish. Arrange fillets on top of mixture, spooning some of mixture on top of fillets. Sprinkle with olive slices. Bake for 20 to 25 minutes, or until fish is firm and opaque and just begins to flake.

Per Serving: Calories: 257 • Protein: 34 g. • Carbohydrate: 8 g. • Fat: 10 g. • Cholesterol: 116 mg. • Sodium: 449 mg. Exchanges: 4 lean meat, 1½ vegetable

Yogurt-Dill Oven-fried Fish ↑

Elizabeth Sexton – Spokane, Washington

½ cup plain nonfat or low-fat yogurt
1 tablespoon snipped fresh dill weed
1 cup crushed seasoned croutons
1½ lbs. any freshwater fish fillets (6 oz. each), skin removed

4 servings

Heat oven to 400°F. Spray large baking sheet with nonstick vegetable cooking spray. Set aside. In shallow dish, combine yogurt and dill. Place crushed croutons in another shallow dish. Dip each fillet first in yogurt mixture and then in crouton crumbs, pressing lightly to coat.

Arrange fillets in single layer on prepared baking sheet. Bake for 25 to 30 minutes, or until fish is firm and opaque and just begins to flake, and coating is golden brown.

Per Serving: Calories: 236 • Protein: 36 g. • Carbohydrate: 12 g. • Fat: 3 g. • Cholesterol: 147 mg. • Sodium: 259 mg.
Exchanges: ¾ starch, 4 lean meat

Perfect Salmon

"This is an old family recipe. I use Walla Walla onions instead of green onions."
Scott M. Burgess – Yakima, Washington

½ cup mayonnaise
½ cup thinly sliced green onions
1 teaspoon prepared mustard
1 salmon, or substitute, fillet (2¼ lbs.), skin on
¼ teaspoon salt
¼ teaspoon pepper
¼ teaspoon garlic powder

6 servings

Spray rack in broiler pan with nonstick vegetable cooking spray. Set aside. In small mixing bowl, combine mayonnaise, onions and mustard. Set aside.

Place fillet skin-side-down on prepared broiler pan. Place under broiler with surface of fish 7 inches from heat. Broil for 10 minutes. Spread mayonnaise mixture evenly on fillet. Sprinkle salt, pepper and garlic powder evenly over mayonnaise mixture. Broil for 10 to 15 minutes, or until fish is firm and opaque and just begins to flake, and mayonnaise mixture is golden brown.

Per Serving: Calories: 376 • Protein: 34 g. • Carbohydrate: 1 g. • Fat: 25 g. • Cholesterol: 104 mg. • Sodium: 280 mg.
Exchanges: 4¾ lean meat, 2 fat

Uchi Lake Pizza Northern

"This is an original recipe that we serve for lunch after a morning of fishing. Our guests love it."
Judy Henrickson, Uchi Lake Lodge – Sioux Lookout, Ontario

1½ lbs. northern pike, or substitute,
    fillets (6 to 8 oz. each), skin
    removed
  1 can (8 oz.) tomato sauce
  2 teaspoons lemon juice
  2 teaspoons Worcestershire sauce
  1 teaspoon dried parsley flakes
  1 teaspoon Italian seasoning
  ¼ teaspoon seasoned salt
  ⅛ teaspoon garlic powder
  1 medium tomato, thinly sliced
  1 small onion, thinly sliced
  1 tablespoon margarine or butter
  ½ cup shredded mozzarella
    cheese

4 servings

Heat oven to 350°F. Cut 22 × 18-inch sheet of heavy-duty foil. Arrange fillets, slightly overlapping, on foil. Set aside. In small mixing bowl, combine tomato sauce, juice, Worcestershire sauce, parsley flakes, Italian seasoning, salt and garlic powder. Spoon mixture evenly over fillets. Arrange tomato and onion slices evenly over fillets. Dot fillets with margarine.

Fold long sides of foil together in locked folds. Fold and crimp short ends; seal tightly. Place packet on large baking sheet. Bake for 30 to 35 minutes, or until fish is firm and opaque and just begins to flake. Open foil during last 10 minutes. Sprinkle with cheese. Return to oven, uncovered, to melt cheese.

Per Serving: Calories: 246 • Protein: 37 g. • Carbohydrate: 8 g. • Fat: 7 g.
• Cholesterol: 77 mg. • Sodium: 606 mg.
Exchanges: 5 lean meat, 1 vegetable

Cheesy Walleye Bake

Julie Zak – Egg Harbor, Wisconsin

10 oz. fresh asparagus spears, cut into 1-inch pieces (2 1/2 cups)
1 1/2 lbs. walleye, or substitute, fillets (6 oz. each), skin removed
1/4 cup plus 2 tablespoons margarine or butter, divided
1 medium onion, finely chopped (1 cup)
1/3 cup all-purpose flour
1 cup milk
1 1/3 cups shredded Cheddar cheese
1/4 teaspoon salt
1/4 teaspoon pepper
1 cup crushed soda crackers

4 to 6 servings

Heat oven to 350°F. Spread asparagus evenly over bottom of 10 × 6-inch baking dish. Arrange fillets, slightly overlapping, on top of asparagus. Set aside.

In 1-quart saucepan, melt 3 tablespoons margarine over medium-low heat. Add onion. Cook for 3 to 5 minutes, or until tender. Stir in flour. Cook for 2 minutes, stirring constantly. Blend in milk. Cook for 3 to 5 minutes, or until mixture thickens and bubbles, stirring constantly. Add cheese, salt and pepper. Remove from heat. Stir until cheese is melted. Spoon cheese sauce mixture evenly over fish fillets.

In 1-quart saucepan, melt remaining 3 tablespoons margarine over medium heat. Remove from heat. Add cracker crumbs, stirring to coat. Sprinkle crumb mixture evenly over cheese sauce. Bake for 40 to 45 minutes, or until sauce is hot and bubbly and fish is firm and opaque and just begins to flake. Let stand for 10 minutes before serving.

Per Serving: Calories: 429 • Protein: 33 g. • Carbohydrate: 20 g. • Fat: 24 g. • Cholesterol: 130 mg. • Sodium: 587 mg. Exchanges: 1 starch, 4 lean meat, 1/4 skim milk, 2 1/2 fat

Baked Fish Elégant

Ellen Knee – Natrona Heights, Pennsylvania

1 1/2 lbs. any freshwater fish fillets (6 oz. each), skin removed
1 bottle (16 oz.) Newman's Own® olive oil and vinegar salad dressing
1 tablespoon white wine Worcestershire sauce

1/2 cup seasoned dry bread crumbs
1 1/2 teaspoons lemon pepper
1 1/2 teaspoons dried tarragon leaves
2 tablespoons margarine or butter
3/4 cup shredded cheese (Monterey Jack, mozzarella or Colby)

4 servings

Arrange fillets, slightly overlapping, in 13 × 9-inch baking dish. Pour dressing over fillets. Cover with plastic wrap. Chill 4 hours.

Heat oven to 350°F. Spray large baking sheet with nonstick vegetable cooking spray. Drain and discard dressing from fillets. Arrange fillets in single layer on prepared baking sheet. Rub fillets evenly with Worcestershire sauce.

In small mixing bowl, combine crumbs, lemon pepper and tarragon. Sprinkle crumb mixture evenly over fillets. Dot with margarine. Sprinkle cheese evenly over fillets. Bake for 20 to 25 minutes, or until fish is firm and opaque and just begins to flake, and cheese is golden brown.

Per Serving: Calories: 428 • Protein: 40 g. • Carbohydrate: 12 g. • Fat: 24 g. • Cholesterol: 166 mg. • Sodium: 1079 mg. Exchanges: 3/4 starch, 5 lean meat, 1 1/2 fat

Crispy Baked Salmon

Elinor Klivans – Camden, Maine

¼ cup ready-to-serve chicken broth or water

2 lbs. salmon, or substitute, fillets (8 oz. each), skin on

¼ cup margarine or butter, melted, divided

1 cup unseasoned dry bread crumbs

¼ cup plus 2 tablespoons ground blanched almonds

2 teaspoons grated lemon peel

1 tablespoon plus 1 teaspoon lemon juice

¼ teaspoon salt

¼ teaspoon pepper

¼ cup sliced almonds

4 servings

Heat oven to 375°F. Spray 11 × 7-inch baking dish with nonstick vegetable cooking spray. Pour broth into prepared dish. Arrange salmon fillets skin-sides-down in prepared dish. Set aside.

In medium mixing bowl, combine 1 tablespoon margarine, the bread crumbs, ground almonds, peel, juice, salt and pepper. Set aside.

Brush fillets with 1 tablespoon remaining margarine. Pat crumb mixture evenly on fillets. Drizzle with 1 tablespoon remaining margarine. Sprinkle almond slices evenly over crumb mixture.

Bake, uncovered, for 10 minutes. Drizzle with remaining 1 tablespoon margarine. Bake for 15 to 20 minutes, or until fish is firm and opaque and just begins to flake, and topping is golden brown.

Per Serving: Calories: 642 • Protein: 52 g. • Carbohydrate: 23 g. • Fat: 37 g.
• Cholesterol: 126 mg. • Sodium: 617 mg.
Exchanges: 1½ starch, 7 lean meat, 3 fat

Fillet of Pike Nicole

Jude W. Theriot – Lake Charles, Louisiana

1 teaspoon salt
½ teaspoon onion powder
¼ to ½ teaspoon cayenne
2¼ lbs. northern pike, or substitute, fillets
  (6 oz. each), skin removed
3 tablespoons olive oil
2 large yellow peppers, cut into thin strips
1 medium onion, chopped (1 cup)
2 large cloves garlic, minced
2 medium tomatoes, peeled, seeded and sliced
¼ teaspoon red pepper sauce
⅓ cup snipped fresh basil leaves

6 servings

Heat oven to 350°F. In small bowl, combine salt, onion powder and cayenne. Set seasoning mixture aside. Spray 13 × 9-inch baking dish with nonstick vegetable cooking spray. Arrange fillets, slightly overlapping, in prepared dish. Sprinkle evenly with seasoning mixture. Set aside.

In 10-inch skillet, heat oil over medium-low heat. Add peppers, onion and garlic. Cook for 5 to 7 minutes, or until vegetables are tender-crisp. Add tomatoes. Cook for 2 to 3 minutes, or until hot. Stir in red pepper sauce and basil. Remove vegetable mixture from heat. Spoon evenly over fillets. Bake, uncovered, for 20 to 25 minutes, or until fish is firm and opaque and just begins to flake.

Per Serving: Calories: 258 • Protein: 38 g. • Carbohydrate: 7 g.
• Fat: 8 g. • Cholesterol: 74 mg. • Sodium: 451 mg.
Exchanges: 5 lean meat, 1 vegetable

Oven-fried Fish

Bill F. Fillmore – Richfield, Minnesota

½ cup unseasoned dry bread crumbs
½ cup crushed sour cream and chive or barbecue-flavored potato chips
½ cup crushed soda crackers
¼ cup shredded fresh Parmesan cheese
2 tablespoons dried parsley flakes
½ teaspoon onion powder
½ teaspoon paprika
½ teaspoon garlic powder
½ teaspoon salt (optional)
½ teaspoon pepper
⅔ cup all-purpose flour
2 eggs, beaten
½ cup milk
1½ lbs. crappie, or substitute, fillets (2 to 3 oz. each), skin removed
½ cup margarine or butter, melted

4 servings

Heat oven to 350°F. In food processor, combine bread crumbs, chips, crackers, Parmesan cheese, parsley, onion powder, paprika, garlic powder, salt and pepper. Pulse 3 or 4 times, or until mixture is fine. Pour crumb mixture into shallow dish. Place flour in another shallow dish. In medium mixing bowl, combine eggs and milk. Set aside.

Spray 13 × 9-inch baking dish with nonstick vegetable cooking spray. Dredge fillets first in flour, then dip in egg mixture and then dredge in crumb mixture to coat. Arrange fillets, slightly overlapping, in prepared dish. Drizzle margarine evenly over fillets. Bake for 25 to 35 minutes, or until fish is firm and opaque and just begins to flake, and coating is golden brown.

Per Serving: Calories: 647 • Protein: 45 g. • Carbohydrate: 38 g. • Fat: 34 g. • Cholesterol: 230 mg. • Sodium: 808 mg. Exchanges: 2½ starch, 5 lean meat, 3¾ fat

Baked Stuffed Bass ↑

Peter F. Scheidel – Unionville, Connecticut

1 pkg. (6 oz.) wild rice and mushroom stuffing mix
¼ cup margarine or butter
¼ cup all-purpose flour
½ teaspoon salt
⅛ teaspoon white pepper
2 cups milk or half-and-half
1½ lbs. bass, or substitute, fillets (6 oz. each), skin removed, cut in half crosswise, ¼ inch thick*

1 tablespoon lemon juice
½ teaspoon grated orange peel
2 tablespoons finely chopped almonds
2 tablespoons grated Parmesan cheese
1 tablespoon snipped fresh parsley

6 servings

Heat oven to 350°F. Prepare stuffing as directed on package. Set aside to cool. In 1-quart saucepan, melt margarine over medium-low heat. Cook just until margarine begins to brown, stirring constantly. Remove from heat. Stir in flour, salt and pepper. Stir until mixture is smooth. Blend in milk. Return to heat. Bring mixture to boil over medium heat, stirring constantly. Reduce heat to low. Simmer for 3 to 4 minutes, or until mixture thickens and bubbles. Remove from heat. Set white sauce aside.

Spray 13 × 9-inch baking dish with nonstick vegetable cooking spray. Spread stuffing evenly over one side of each fillet. Roll up each fillet and secure with wooden picks. Arrange in prepared dish. Sprinkle evenly with juice and peel. Spoon white sauce evenly over fish. Sprinkle evenly with almonds, Parmesan cheese and parsley. Bake for 25 to 30 minutes, or until fish is firm and opaque and just begins to flake.

*Thick fillets may be cut in half horizontally to yield ¼-inch-thick fillets.

Per Serving: Calories: 522 • Protein: 30 g. • Carbohydrate: 26 g. • Fat: 33 g. • Cholesterol: 90 mg. • Sodium: 867 mg. Exchanges: 1½ starch, 3½ lean meat, ⅓ skim milk, 4½ fat

Oriental Fish Bake ↑

Charles E. Nitschke – New York Mills, Minnesota

1 tablespoon salt-free herb and spice blend
1 teaspoon onion powder
1 teaspoon garlic powder
1/2 teaspoon salt
1/4 to 1/2 teaspoon pepper
1/4 teaspoon cayenne
2 northern pike, or substitute, fillets (18 oz. each),
   skin removed
1 can (16 oz.) Oriental vegetables, rinsed and well
   drained
1/2 cup thinly sliced green onions
1/4 cup soy sauce

6 servings

Heat oven to 325°F. Cut 20 × 18-inch sheet of heavy-duty foil. Place foil in 13 × 9-inch baking dish, with ends hanging over. Set aside.

In small bowl, combine seasonings. Sprinkle seasoning mixture evenly over one side of each fillet. Place 1 fillet seasoned-side-up in foil-lined dish. Top with Oriental vegetables and onions. Sprinkle with soy sauce. Place remaining fillet seasoned-side-up on vegetables.

Fold long sides of foil together in locked folds. Fold and crimp short ends; seal tightly. Bake for 40 to 45 minutes, or until fish is firm and opaque and just begins to flake.

Per Serving: Calories: 179 • Protein: 35 g. • Carbohydrate: 5 g. • Fat: 1 g. • Cholesterol: 66 mg. • Sodium: 944 mg.
Exchanges: 4 lean meat, 1 vegetable

Lime-broiled Fish

Gloria Rose – Springfield, New Jersey

1/4 cup fresh lime juice
2 tablespoons plus 1 teaspoon Dijon mustard,
   divided
2 teaspoons freshly grated gingerroot
2 teaspoons frozen apple juice concentrate,
   defrosted
1/8 teaspoon cayenne
   Dash pepper
1 1/2 lbs. any freshwater fish fillets (6 oz. each),
   skin removed

4 servings

In 13 × 9-inch baking dish, combine lime juice, 1 teaspoon mustard, the gingerroot, apple juice concentrate, cayenne and pepper. Arrange fillets, slightly overlapping, in dish, turning to coat. Cover with plastic wrap. Chill 1/2 hour, turning fillets over once.

Drain and discard marinade from fillets. Spray rack in broiler pan with nonstick vegetable cooking spray. Arrange fillets on prepared broiler pan. Brush remaining 2 tablespoons mustard evenly over fillets. Place under broiler with surface of fish 6 inches from heat. Broil for 8 to 10 minutes, or until fish is firm and opaque and just begins to flake, and mustard browns slightly. Garnish with sliced green onions, if desired.

Per Serving: Calories: 175 • Protein: 33 g. • Carbohydrate: 2 g. • Fat: 3 g. • Cholesterol: 146 mg. • Sodium: 331 mg.
Exchanges: 4 lean meat

Baked Fish Fillets with Hot Tomato Salsa

Vicki M. Lavorini – San Francisco, California

1½ lbs. walleye, or substitute,
    fillets (6 oz. each), skin
    removed
¼ teaspoon salt
¼ teaspoon pepper
1 can (16 oz.) stewed tomatoes,
    drained
¼ cup hot or medium salsa
3 tablespoons tomato paste

4 servings

Heat oven to 400°F. Spray 11 × 7-inch baking dish with nonstick vegetable cooking spray. Arrange fillets, slightly overlapping, in prepared dish. Sprinkle evenly with salt and pepper. Set aside.

In small mixing bowl, combine tomatoes, salsa and tomato paste. Spoon mixture evenly over fillets. Cover dish with foil. Bake for 35 to 40 minutes, or until fish is firm and opaque and just begins to flake. Garnish with lemon wedges and serve over rice, if desired.

Per Serving: Calories: 202 • Protein: 34 g. • Carbohydrate: 11 g. • Fat: 2 g.
• Cholesterol: 146 mg. • Sodium: 697 mg.
Exchanges: 3 lean meat, 2 vegetable

Fish Cheese Puff

"Mom's recipe is so good!"
David Anthony Woellner – Auburndale, Wisconsin

2¼ lbs. northern pike, or substitute, fillets (6 oz.
   each), skin removed
½ cup sour cream
½ cup shredded Cheddar cheese
2 eggs, separated
2 tablespoons sliced pimiento-stuffed green olives
1 tablespoon finely chopped onion
¼ teaspoon salt

6 servings

Heat oven to 350°F. Spray 11 × 7-inch baking dish with nonstick vegetable cooking spray. Arrange fillets, slightly overlapping, in prepared dish. Set aside.

In large mixing bowl, combine sour cream, cheese, egg yolks, olives, onion and salt. Set aside.

In medium mixing bowl, beat egg whites at high speed of electric mixer until stiff but not dry. Gently fold egg whites into sour cream mixture. Spread mixture evenly over fillets. Bake for 25 to 30 minutes, or until fish is firm and opaque and just begins to flake, and puff is light golden brown.

Per Serving: Calories: 259 • Protein: 38 g. • Carbohydrate: 1 g. • Fat: 10 g. • Cholesterol: 156 mg. • Sodium: 314 mg. Exchanges: 5 lean meat

Whitefish Bake →

Elinor B. Williams – Keene, New Hampshire

¼ cup margarine or butter
8 to 10 new potatoes, thinly sliced (about 1 lb.)
1 large onion, chopped (2 cups)
1 cup chopped green pepper
1 large clove garlic, minced
1 teaspoon ground thyme
½ teaspoon salt
¼ teaspoon pepper
1½ lbs. whitefish, or substitute, fillets (6 oz. each), skin removed
2 medium tomatoes, each cut into 8 wedges

4 to 6 servings

Heat oven to 400°F. In 12-inch skillet, melt margarine over medium heat. Add potatoes, onion, green pepper, garlic and seasonings. Cook for 6 to 10 minutes, or until tender-crisp, stirring frequently. Remove from heat. Set aside.

Spray 13 × 9-inch baking dish with nonstick vegetable cooking spray. Arrange fillets, slightly overlapping, in prepared dish. Top evenly with vegetable mixture. Arrange tomatoes evenly over vegetables. Bake for 40 to 45 minutes, or until fish is firm and opaque and just begins to flake, and potatoes are tender.

Per Serving: Calories: 314 • Protein: 24 g. • Carbohydrate: 21 g. • Fat: 15 g. • Cholesterol: 68 mg. • Sodium: 340 mg. Exchanges: 1 starch, 3 lean meat, 1 vegetable, 1¼ fat

Catfish Christine

Jude W. Theriot – Lake Charles, Louisiana

1 can (14½ oz.) ready-to-serve chicken broth
1 cup dry white wine
2 pkgs. (9 oz. each) frozen chopped spinach
½ teaspoon red pepper sauce
¼ cup unsalted margarine or butter
3 tablespoons all-purpose flour
½ cup whipping cream
⅔ cup shredded Swiss cheese
½ teaspoon salt
¼ teaspoon white pepper
2¼ lbs. catfish fillets (6 oz. each), skin removed
¼ cup freshly grated Romano cheese

6 servings

In 2-quart saucepan, bring broth and wine to boil over medium heat. Add spinach and red pepper sauce. Reduce heat to low. Cook, uncovered, for 20 minutes, or until spinach is hot, stirring once or twice.

Heat oven to 375°F. Drain spinach over 4-cup measure, pressing to remove excess moisture. Reserve 1 cup drained liquid. Set spinach and reserved liquid aside. Discard remaining liquid.

In same 2-quart saucepan, melt margarine over medium-low heat. Gradually stir in flour. Cook for 4 to 5 minutes, or until light golden brown, stirring constantly. Gradually stir in reserved liquid. Cook for 5 to 7 minutes, or until sauce thickens and bubbles, stirring constantly. Blend in cream, Swiss cheese, salt and pepper. Stir until cheese is melted. Remove from heat. Set aside.

Spray 13 × 9-inch baking dish with nonstick vegetable cooking spray. Arrange fillets, slightly overlapping, in prepared dish. Pour half of sauce (about 1 cup) evenly over fillets. Bake, uncovered, for 5 minutes. In medium mixing bowl, combine remaining sauce and the spinach. Spread spinach mixture evenly over fish. Sprinkle with Romano cheese. Bake for 20 to 25 minutes, or until fish is firm and opaque and just begins to flake.

Per Serving: Calories: 433 • Protein: 39 g. • Carbohydrate: 8 g. • Fat: 27 g. • Cholesterol: 162 mg. • Sodium: 565 mg. Exchanges: ¼ starch, 5 lean meat, 1 vegetable, 2½ fat

Oven-fried Pike with Orange Sauce ↑

Gayetta Quenemoen – Great Falls, Montana

1½ lbs. northern pike, or substitute, fillets (6 oz. each), skin removed, cut in half crosswise	¼ cup vegetable oil, divided
1 cup orange juice	½ teaspoon ground ginger
¼ cup thinly sliced green onions	¼ teaspoon salt
2 tablespoons lemon juice	½ cup all-purpose flour
	1 tablespoon lemon herb seasoning

4 servings

Place fillets in large plastic food-storage bag. Set aside. In 2-cup measure, combine orange juice, onions, lemon juice, 2 tablespoons oil, the ginger and salt. Reserve half of juice mixture. Cover and chill. Pour remaining juice mixture over fillets. Secure bag. Turn to coat. Chill ½ hour, turning bag once.

Pour remaining 2 tablespoons oil in 13 × 9-inch baking pan, tilting pan to coat bottom with oil. Heat oven to 450°F. Heat oil in oven for 10 to 15 minutes, or until very hot. In shallow dish, combine flour and lemon herb seasoning. Drain and discard juice mixture from fillets. Blot excess moisture from fillets with paper towels. Dredge both sides of fillets in flour mixture to coat. Place in hot oil in pan. Bake for 8 to 10 minutes, or until bottoms of fillets are browned. Turn fillets over. Bake for 5 to 6 minutes longer, or until browned on both sides.

Meanwhile, place reserved juice mixture in 1-quart saucepan. Simmer over medium heat for 10 to 12 minutes, or until reduced by half. Pour sauce over fillets. Garnish with orange slices and snipped fresh parsley, if desired.

Per Serving: Calories: 368 • Protein: 35 g. • Carbohydrate: 22 g. • Fat: 15 g.
• Cholesterol: 66 mg. • Sodium: 208 mg.
Exchanges: ¾ starch, 4½ lean meat, ¾ fruit, ¼ fat

Jo's Bass Bake

"This is a meal in itself. Serve with melon balls, a good white wine or iced tea."
  Joan Alvers – Zion, Illinois

2 cups uncooked brown rice
4 cups water
¼ cup plus 2 tablespoons margarine or butter, divided
1 teaspoon salt
8 oz. fresh mushrooms, sliced (2 cups)
2 cups thinly sliced carrots
1 medium red pepper, chopped (1 cup)
1 medium green pepper, chopped (1 cup)
1 medium onion, chopped (1 cup)
1 teaspoon dried thyme leaves (optional)
1½ lbs. bass, or substitute, fillets (6 oz. each), skin removed
1 can (14½ oz.) ready-to-serve chicken broth

4 to 6 servings

Grease 13 × 9-inch baking dish. Set aside. In 3-quart saucepan, combine rice, water, 2 tablespoons margarine and the salt. Bring mixture to boil over medium-high heat. Reduce heat to low. Cover. Cook for 40 to 50 minutes, or until liquid is absorbed and rice is tender. Set aside.

Heat oven to 375°F. In 12-inch skillet, melt remaining ¼ cup margarine over medium-high heat. Add vegetables and thyme. Cook mixture for 10 to 15 minutes, or until vegetables are tender-crisp, stirring frequently.

Spoon half of rice (about 3½ cups) into prepared dish. Spread rice into even layer, packing with back of spoon. Spread vegetable mixture in even layer over rice. Arrange fillets, slightly overlapping, over vegetables. Top with remaining rice, spreading and packing with back of spoon to form even layer. Pour broth evenly over rice. Bake for 45 minutes to 1 hour, or until hot and bubbly around edges.

Per Serving: Calories: 511 • Protein: 29 g.
• Carbohydrate: 57 g. • Fat: 18 g.
• Cholesterol: 77 mg. • Sodium: 898 mg.
Exchanges: 3 starch, 3 lean meat,
1 vegetable, 2 fat

Catfish Pot Pie

Thomas K. Squier – Aberdeen, North Carolina

 3   slices bacon
1½   lbs. catfish fillets (6 oz. each), skin removed,
       cut into 1-inch pieces
 2   cups frozen mixed vegetables
 1   cup chopped onions
 1   cup thinly sliced celery
 4   oz. fresh mushrooms, sliced (1 cup)
 3   tablespoons all-purpose flour
 1   teaspoon salt
 ½   teaspoon pepper
 ½   teaspoon dried thyme leaves

TOPPING:
 2   cups buttermilk baking mix
 1   cup milk

4 to 6 servings

Heat oven to 400°F. In 10-inch skillet, cook bacon over medium heat until brown and crisp. Drain on paper-towel-lined plate. Crumble bacon. In medium mixing bowl, combine bacon and remaining ingredients, except topping. Spray 13 × 9-inch baking dish with nonstick vegetable cooking spray. Spoon fish and vegetable mixture evenly into prepared dish. Set aside.

In medium mixing bowl, combine topping ingredients. Spoon batter evenly over fish mixture, spreading to edges. Bake for 30 to 35 minutes, or until crust is golden brown.

Per Serving: Calories: 401 • Protein: 29 g. • Carbohydrate: 41 g. • Fat: 13 g. • Cholesterol: 74 mg. • Sodium: 1022 mg. Exchanges: 2¼ starch, 3 lean meat, 1½ vegetable, 1 fat

Cornish Striper Pasties

Annette Bignami – Moscow, Idaho

PASTRY:
- 4½ cups all-purpose flour
- 1 teaspoon salt
- 1 teaspoon curry powder
- ¼ teaspoon paprika
- 1½ cups shortening
- ¾ cup ice water

- 2 cups flaked cooked striped bass or substitute (about 1 lb.)
- 1½ cups cubed red potatoes (¼-inch cubes)

- ¾ cup thinly sliced carrot
- ¾ cup chopped onion
- 2 tablespoons plus 2 teaspoons sherry
- ½ teaspoon dried thyme leaves
- ⅛ teaspoon salt
- ⅛ teaspoon pepper
- 1 tablespoon all-purpose flour
- ½ teaspoon sugar
- 1 medium red or green cooking apple (8 oz.), cored and cut into ½-inch cubes

EGG WASH:
- 1 egg, beaten with 2 tablespoons water

6 servings

Per Serving: Calories: 974 • Protein: 29 g. • Carbohydrate: 89 g. • Fat: 55 g. • Cholesterol: 111 mg. • Sodium: 500 mg. Exchanges: 5 starch, 3 lean meat, ½ vegetable, ½ fruit, 9 fat

How to Make Cornish Striper Pasties

COMBINE all pastry ingredients, except shortening and water, in large mixing bowl. Cut in shortening to form coarse crumbs.

SPRINKLE with water, 1 tablespoon at a time, mixing with fork until particles are moistened and cling together.

FORM dough into ball. Wrap with plastic wrap. Chill 30 minutes.

HEAT oven to 350°F. In another large mixing bowl, combine bass, potatoes, carrot, onion, sherry, thyme, salt and pepper. Set aside.

COMBINE 1 tablespoon flour and the sugar in medium mixing bowl. Add apple. Stir to coat. Set aside.

DIVIDE dough into 12 equal pieces. Place 2 pieces on lightly floured board. (Keep remaining pieces covered with plastic wrap.)

ROLL each piece to 7-inch-diameter circle. Place 1 scant cup of fish mixture on center of one circle, leaving 1-inch border. Top with ¼ cup apple mixture.

BRUSH egg wash around edge of dough. Top with remaining dough circle. Press edges together with tines of fork to seal.

PLACE on ungreased baking sheet. Repeat with remaining dough, filling and apples. Bake for 40 to 45 minutes, or until crust is lightly browned.

96

D. J.'s Ice-fishing Casserole

"This is my husband's favorite meal when he comes home from a day of ice fishing."
Darla J. Wood – Burghill, Ohio

7 to 8 medium red potatoes, peeled and thinly
    sliced (5 cups)
¼ cup water
¼ cup margarine or butter
½ cup all-purpose flour
1 teaspoon instant minced onion
½ teaspoon garlic powder
½ teaspoon salt
¼ teaspoon pepper
2 cups milk
2 cups shredded Cheddar cheese
2 cups frozen broccoli cuts
1 lb. walleye, or substitute, fillets (6 to 8 oz. each),
    skin removed, cut into 1-inch pieces
    Paprika

4 to 6 servings

Heat conventional oven to 350°F. In 3-quart casserole, combine potatoes and water. Cover. Microwave at High for 10 to 13 minutes, or until potatoes are tender-crisp, stirring twice. Drain. Set aside.

In 4-cup measure, microwave margarine at High for 1¼ to 1½ minutes, or until melted. Stir in flour, minced onion, garlic powder, salt and pepper. Blend in milk. Microwave at High for 5 to 7 minutes, or until mixture thickens and bubbles, stirring every 2 minutes. Stir in cheese until melted.

Pour cheese mixture over potatoes. Mix well. Add broccoli and fish pieces. Stir gently to coat. Sprinkle with paprika. Bake conventionally, uncovered, for 1 hour to 1 hour 10 minutes, or until hot and bubbly and browned on top.

Per Serving: Calories: 488 • Protein: 31 g. • Carbohydrate: 37 g. • Fat: 24 g. • Cholesterol: 116 mg. • Sodium: 601 mg.
Exchanges: 2 starch, 3 lean meat, ¼ vegetable, ½ skim milk, 3 fat

Easy Fish Loaf ↑

Joan Cone – Williamsburg, Virginia

1 egg, beaten
¼ cup half-and-half
2 cups flaked cooked yellow perch or substitute (about 1 lb.)
¾ cup unseasoned dry bread crumbs
2 tablespoons snipped fresh parsley
1 tablespoon margarine or butter, melted
1 tablespoon lemon juice
1 teaspoon instant minced onion
½ teaspoon salt
¼ teaspoon paprika

4 servings

Heat oven to 400°F. In medium mixing bowl, combine egg and half-and-half. Stir in remaining ingredients. Spray 8 × 4-inch loaf pan with nonstick vegetable cooking spray. Spoon mixture into prepared pan, packing lightly. Bake for 20 to 25 minutes, or until internal temperature registers 150°F. Loosen edges with knife. Invert on serving platter. Serve immediately. Serve with tartar sauce, if desired.

Per Serving: Calories: 273 • Protein: 33 g.
• Carbohydrate: 15 g. • Fat: 8 g.
• Cholesterol: 190 mg. • Sodium: 558 mg.
Exchanges: 1 starch, 4 lean meat

Deep-dish Crayfish Pie

Keith Sutton – Benton, Arkansas

½ cup margarine or butter
1 cup chopped onions
½ cup chopped green pepper
½ cup chopped celery
2 cloves garlic, minced
1 tablespoon paprika
1 tablespoon Worcestershire sauce
½ teaspoon salt
¼ teaspoon cayenne
¼ teaspoon pepper
1 can (10¾ oz.) condensed cream of chicken soup

1⅓ cups water, divided
2 tablespoons cornstarch
1 cup unseasoned dry bread crumbs
1 lb. steamed peeled crayfish tails Pastry for double-crust deep-dish pie

EGG WASH:
1 egg yolk, beaten with 2 tablespoons water

6 to 8 servings

Heat oven to 400°F. In 4-quart Dutch oven or stockpot, melt margarine over medium-low heat. Add onions, green pepper and celery. Cook for 5 to 6 minutes, or until vegetables are tender-crisp. Stir in garlic, paprika, Worcestershire sauce, salt, cayenne and pepper. Blend in soup and ⅔ cup water. Bring mixture to simmer over medium heat, stirring occasionally.

In small mixing bowl, combine remaining ⅔ cup water and the cornstarch. Stir into vegetable mixture. Cook over medium heat for 1 to 2 minutes, or until mixture is thickened, stirring constantly. Remove from heat. Stir in bread crumbs and crayfish. Set aside.

Ease crust into 10-inch deep-dish pie plate, leaving 1-inch overhang. Spoon crayfish mixture evenly into crust. Cover with second crust. Roll top and bottom crusts together to seal. Flute edge. Cut slits in top crust to vent. Brush crust with egg wash. Bake for 15 minutes. Reduce heat to 350°F. Bake for 20 to 25 minutes longer, or until crust is golden brown.

Per Serving: Calories: 506 • Protein: 20 g. • Carbohydrate: 37 g. • Fat: 31 g.
• Cholesterol: 131 mg. • Sodium: 1005 mg.
Exchanges: 2 starch, 2 lean meat, 1 vegetable, 5 fat

Delicious Turtle

Mildred Floding – Alexandria, Minnesota

 1   cup all-purpose flour
1½ teaspoons paprika
 ¾   teaspoon salt
 ¼   teaspoon pepper
2¼ lbs. snapping turtle meat, trimmed and cut into
       1-inch cubes
 ¼   cup plus 2 tablespoons margarine or butter
 1   can (12 oz.) evaporated milk
 1   can (10¾ oz.) condensed cream of mushroom
       soup
 1   can (10¾ oz.) condensed cream of chicken soup
 1   cup water
 2   tablespoons snipped fresh parsley

6 to 8 servings

Heat oven to 325°F. In medium mixing bowl, combine flour, paprika, salt and pepper. Dredge turtle meat in flour mixture to coat.

In 12-inch skillet, melt margarine over medium-low heat. Add turtle pieces. Cook for 3 to 4 minutes, or until browned. Remove from heat. Spray 3-quart casserole with nonstick vegetable cooking spray. Spoon turtle meat into prepared casserole. Set aside.

In medium mixing bowl, combine milk, soups, water and parsley. Pour mixture over turtle meat. Stir to coat. Bake, covered, for 2 to 3 hours, or until turtle meat is tender, stirring once or twice.

Nutritional information not available.

← Turtle Stroganoff

Jim Schneider – New Ulm, Minnesota

 ½   cup all-purpose flour
1½ lbs. snapping turtle meat, trimmed and cut into
       1-inch cubes
 ¼   cup vegetable oil, divided
 2   tablespoons margarine or butter
 1   medium onion, cut in half and thinly sliced
 1   can (10½ oz.) condensed beef broth
 ¾   cup red wine
 2   tablespoons soy sauce
 1   tablespoon ground ginger
 1   tablespoon Worcestershire sauce
 1   bay leaf

MARINADE:
 2   tablespoons soy sauce
 1   tablespoon margarine or butter, melted
 1   tablespoon vegetable oil
 1   teaspoon ground ginger
 1   teaspoon instant minced onion
 1   teaspoon Worcestershire sauce
       Pinch sugar

 1   lb. fresh mushrooms, thinly sliced (4 cups)
 1   pkg. (10 oz.) uncooked wide egg noodles
       Snipped fresh parsley

4 to 6 servings

Heat oven to 325°F. Place flour in shallow dish. Dredge turtle meat in flour to coat. In 4-quart Dutch oven or stockpot, heat 3 tablespoons oil over medium heat. Add turtle meat. Cook for 3 to 4 minutes, or until browned. Remove meat from Dutch oven. Set aside.

Spray 3-quart casserole with nonstick vegetable cooking spray. Set aside. In same Dutch oven, melt 2 tablespoons margarine over medium heat. Add onion. Cook for 2 to 3 minutes, or until tender, stirring frequently. Stir in broth, wine, soy sauce, ginger, Worcestershire sauce and bay leaf. Bring mixture to boil. Add turtle meat. Remove from heat. Transfer mixture to prepared casserole. Bake, covered, for 45 to 50 minutes, or until turtle meat is tender, removing cover during last 15 minutes.

Reduce oven temperature to 175°F. Re-cover casserole. Keep warm in oven. In medium mixing bowl, combine marinade ingredients. Add mushrooms and toss to coat. Set aside. Prepare noodles as directed on package. Drain. Cover to keep warm. Set aside.

In 12-inch skillet, heat remaining 1 tablespoon oil over medium heat. Add mushroom mixture. Cook for 4 to 5 minutes, or until mushrooms are tender, stirring frequently. Add mushroom mixture to turtle mixture. Mix well. Place noodles on large serving platter. Spoon turtle mixture evenly over noodles. Garnish with snipped fresh parsley.

Nutritional information not available.

Cheesy Bacon-baked Trout Spread

Judy M. Claffy – Reno, Nevada

4 slices bacon, finely chopped
1 whole drawn stream trout (8 oz.)
1 pkg. (8 oz.) cream cheese, softened
1 cup shredded Cheddar cheese
½ cup sliced green onions
½ cup sour cream
¼ teaspoon garlic powder
1 tablespoon milk

2½ cups, 20 servings

Heat oven to 350°F. In 8-inch skillet, cook bacon over medium heat until brown and crisp. Drain on paper-towel-lined plate. Cut 18 × 18-inch sheet of heavy-duty foil. Place trout on foil. Stuff cavity of fish with half of bacon. Sprinkle remaining bacon over fish.

Fold long sides of foil together in locked folds. Fold and crimp short ends; seal tightly. Bake for 25 to 30 minutes, or until fish begins to flake when fork is inserted at backbone in thickest part of fish. Set aside to cool.

In medium mixing bowl, combine remaining ingredients. Remove bacon from fish. Add to cream cheese mixture. Remove skin and bones from fish. Flake fish and add to cream cheese mixture. Mix well. Cover with plastic wrap. Chill 2 hours. Serve with crackers.

Per Serving: Calories: 91 • Protein: 4 g. • Carbohydrate: 1 g.
• Fat: 8 g. • Cholesterol: 26 mg. • Sodium: 94 mg.
Exchanges: 1½ medium-fat meat, ¼ vegetable, 1 fat

Easy Trout Dip ↑

Keith Sutton – Benton, Arkansas

2 whole drawn stream trout (8 oz. each)
2 teaspoons lemon juice
1 tablespoon plus 2 teaspoons soy sauce, divided
1 small onion, thinly sliced
½ cup finely chopped onion
½ cup sweet pickle relish
3 hard-cooked eggs, chopped and divided
⅔ cup salad dressing or mayonnaise

3 cups, 24 servings

Heat oven to 350°F. Rub cavities of trout evenly with juice and 2 teaspoons soy sauce. Stuff cavities evenly with onion slices. Spray 10 × 6-inch baking dish with nonstick vegetable cooking spray. Arrange trout in prepared dish. Bake for 20 to 25 minutes, or until fish begins to flake when fork is inserted at backbone in thickest part of fish. Chill trout at least 1 hour.

Discard onion slices. Remove heads, skin and bones; flake meat. In large mixing bowl, combine fish, remaining 1 tablespoon soy sauce, the chopped onion, relish, 2 chopped hard-cooked eggs and the dressing. Cover with plastic wrap. Chill at least 1 hour. Top with remaining chopped hard-cooked egg. Serve with crackers, chips or vegetables, if desired.

Per Serving: Calories: 58 • Protein: 3 g. • Carbohydrate: 4 g.
• Fat: 3 g. • Cholesterol: 35 mg. • Sodium: 151 mg.
Exchanges: ½ medium-fat meat, ¼ fruit

Techniques for Grilling

Many people do not associate outdoor grilling with fish, but the fact is, grilled fish has the same delicious charred-wood flavor as other grilled meats. Oily fish, such as trout and salmon, are best suited to grilling because they stay moist despite the high-heat cooking process. Lean fish, such as walleye or largemouth bass, tend to get dry unless you select thick cuts.

You can grill steaks, fillets or whole fish. On the average, fish should cook for 10 minutes per inch of thickness.

Any fish can be grilled, but many freshwater species, such as crappie and walleye, have delicate meat that breaks up easily and falls through the grate. Always grill these fish in a grilling basket or on a grilling screen or piece of aluminum foil. Fillets or steaks from firm-textured fish such as northern pike and salmon can be placed directly on a well-oiled grill.

If you place a skin-on fillet or whole fish directly on the grate, the skin may stick. An oil-based marinade not only adds flavor to grilled fish, it prevents lean fish from drying out and reduces the chance that the meat will stick. Coat the fish with marinade before cooking and baste frequently during the cooking process.

Types of Grills

CHARCOAL GRILLS are inexpensive, portable and impart a distinct charred-wood flavor. You can regulate the heat by adjusting the air vents. But they heat up more slowly than gas grills and require more cleanup time.

GAS GRILLS cook the fish over a bed of hot lava rocks. They start easily and heat up quickly, and you can control the temperature by regulating the gas flow. But they're costlier and less portable than charcoal grills.

EQUIPMENT for grilling includes (1) grilling screen and (2) grilling basket, to prevent fish from sticking to the grate; (3) long-handled tongs, for moving coals and turning food over; (4) long-handled spatula, for turning and removing fish from the grill; (5) nonstick vegetable cooking spray, for oiling the grate prior to cooking; (6) heavy-duty aluminum foil, for wrapping fish and to prevent sticking; (7) long-handled basting brush, used to baste the fish with marinades or sauces; (8) fine-mist spray bottle, for controlling flare-ups; (9) electric charcoal starter; (10) liquid charcoal starter and (11) charcoal.

How to Grill Fish *(charcoal grill shown)*

SPRAY the grate with nonstick vegetable cooking spray after cleaning it thoroughly with a stiff wire brush or coarse steel wool and rinsing it with water. Do not spray the grate over hot coals; the spray may ignite.

PILE briquets in a tight mound, douse them with charcoal lighter and ignite; or, use an electric charcoal starter. After the coals turn white, use tongs to spread them in a layer extending about 1 inch beyond the cooking area.

ARRANGE fish on a grilling screen or on pieces of foil. Or, place fish in a greased wire basket before setting it on the grate, to prevent sticking. Steaks or skinned fillets can be cooked directly on the grate, if the meat is firm-textured.

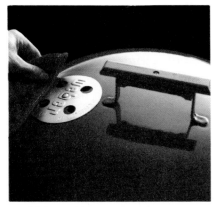

CLOSE the lid and adjust the vents to regulate the heat. You can also increase the heat by lowering the grate or bunching the coals more closely, and you can reduce the heat by raising the grate or spreading the coals.

SPRITZ the coals with a fine mist of water if dripping oil causes a flare-up. You can prevent flare-ups by spreading the coals into piles on opposite sides of the cooking area so the food does not drip directly onto the coals.

TURN the fish after half the cooking time, using a long-handled spatula. Total cooking time depends on air temperature and wind strength, but seldom exceeds 10 minutes per inch of thickness.

Tips for Grilling

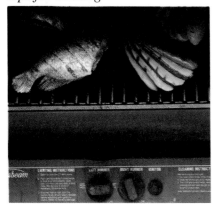

SET one burner of a double-burner gas grill at a lower temperature. This way, you can cook fish over high heat and vegetables over lower heat.

PLACE a pan of soaked wood chips on the lava rocks in a gas grill to add flavor. If you sprinkle chips on the rocks, ash could clog the gas vents.

REMOVE hardened grease from your grate with a foaming-type oven cleaner. Keep the grate clean by washing frequently in soapy water.

Fiesta Grilled Fish ↑

"Goes great with big, whole onions, cooked baked-potato-style."
Patricia M. Shores – Binghamton, New York

    1   whole drawn northern pike or substitute
          (2 to 3 lbs.), scaled, head removed
   1/2 teaspoon salt
   1/2 teaspoon pepper
    1   small lemon, thinly sliced
    1   small lime, thinly sliced
  1 1/2 cups chunky salsa
   1/2 cup beer

4 servings

Prepare grill for low direct heat. Cut 2 sheets of 18-inch heavy-duty foil about 8 inches longer than fish. Sprinkle fish inside and out with salt and pepper. Place fish on 1 sheet of foil. Squeeze 1 slice each of lemon and lime over fish and stuff cavity with remaining slices. Fold sides and ends of foil up slightly around fish. Pour salsa and beer evenly over fish.

Fold long sides of foil together in locked folds. Fold and crimp short ends; seal tightly. Place packet on top of second sheet of foil. Overwrap by bringing long sides of foil together in locked folds. Twist short ends to seal, forming handles for turning packet.

Place packet on cooking grate. Grill, covered, for 15 minutes. Turn packet over. Grill, covered, for 15 to 18 minutes longer, or until fish begins to flake when fork is inserted at backbone in thickest part of fish.

Per Serving: Calories: 185 • Protein: 31 g. • Carbohydrate: 7 g. • Fat: 2 g. • Cholesterol: 137 mg. • Sodium: 896 mg. Exchanges: 4 lean meat, 1 1/2 vegetable

Grilled Lemon Trout with Rosemary

Thomas K. Squier – Aberdeen, North Carolina

MARINADE:
   1/2 cup olive oil
   1/4 cup lemon juice
   1/4 cup snipped fresh rosemary leaves
    3   cloves garlic, minced
   1/4 teaspoon salt
   1/4 teaspoon pepper

    4   whole drawn stream trout (8 oz. each)
    6   to 10 branches wet rosemary
        Lemon wedges

4 servings

In 11 × 7-inch baking dish, combine marinade ingredients. Place trout in baking dish, turning to coat. Cover with plastic wrap. Refrigerate 8 hours or overnight, turning trout over once.

Spray cooking grate with nonstick vegetable cooking spray. Prepare grill for medium direct heat. Drain and discard marinade from fish. Drop a few wet rosemary branches evenly over coals. Arrange trout on prepared cooking grate. Grill, covered, for 8 to 12 minutes, or until fish begins to flake when fork is inserted at backbone in thickest part of fish, turning over once. Continue dropping wet rosemary branches over hot coals to keep smoking constant. Serve with lemon wedges.

Per Serving: Calories: 295 • Protein: 29 g. • Carbohydrate: 2 g. • Fat: 19 g. • Cholesterol: 80 mg. • Sodium: 110 mg. Exchanges: 4 lean meat, 1 1/3 fat

Charcoal-grilled Trout

Richard J. Parmley — St. Louis, Missouri

MARINADE:

- ¼ cup olive oil
- 3 tablespoons fresh lemon juice
- 2 garlic cloves, minced
- 3 fresh basil leaves, finely snipped
- ⅛ teaspoon salt
- ⅛ teaspoon freshly ground pepper
- 2 whole drawn stream trout (8 oz. each)

2 servings

In 11 × 7-inch baking dish, combine marinade ingredients. Place trout in baking dish, turning to coat. Brush some of marinade inside cavity of each fish. Cover with plastic wrap. Chill 2 hours.

Spray cooking grate with nonstick vegetable cooking spray. Prepare grill for high direct heat. Drain and discard marinade from fish.

Arrange trout on prepared cooking grate. Grill, covered, for 8 to 12 minutes, or until fish begins to flake when fork is inserted at backbone in thickest part of fish, turning over once. Garnish each serving with lemon and lime wedges, if desired.

Per Serving: Calories: 299 • Protein: 29 g.
• Carbohydrate: 2 g. • Fat: 19 g.
• Cholesterol: 80 mg. • Sodium: 104 mg.
Exchanges: 4 lean meat, 1½ fat

Poblano Catfish in Leek

"We had picked up a lot of vegetables and some fresh catfish, and just started putting things together. It came out quite well."
Mark S. Peniston – Irving, Texas

2 leeks
1 medium red or green pepper, thinly sliced
1 poblano pepper (1 oz.), seeded and thinly sliced
3 tablespoons fresh cilantro leaves, chopped
2 cloves garlic, thinly sliced
2 small limes, thinly sliced
2 whole drawn catfish (about 1 ¼ lbs. each), head and skin removed
2 teaspoons prepared Cajun seasoning

2 to 3 servings

Per Serving: Calories: 243 • Protein: 30 g.
• Carbohydrate: 16 g. • Fat: 7 g.
• Cholesterol: 90 mg. • Sodium: 671 mg.
Exchanges: 3 lean meat, 3 vegetable

How to Prepare Poblano Catfish in Leek

PREPARE grill for medium-high direct heat. Remove 4 large outer leaves from leeks. Set aside. Cut leeks in half lengthwise; rinse. Chop to equal 1 cup. In medium mixing bowl, combine chopped leeks, pepper slices, cilantro and garlic.

SPRAY 20-inch fish-grilling basket with nonstick vegetable cooking spray. On one side of basket, layer half of reserved leek leaves, half of lime slices and half of pepper mixture.

SPRINKLE both sides of each catfish evenly with Cajun seasoning. Arrange fish in basket. Top with remaining pepper mixture and lime slices. Cover with remaining leek leaves. Secure basket.

PLACE basket on cooking grate. Grill, covered, for 15 minutes. Turn basket over. Grill, covered, for 15 to 20 minutes longer, or until fish begins to flake when fork is inserted at backbone in thickest part of fish.

Butterflied Barbecued Northern ↑

Thomas K. Squier – Aberdeen, North Carolina

SAUCE:

- ¼ cup tomato paste
- 2 tablespoons water
- 1 tablespoon fresh lime juice
- 1 tablespoon Worcestershire sauce
- 1 tablespoon molasses
- 1½ teaspoons olive oil
- ½ teaspoon salt
- ⅛ teaspoon garlic powder

- 1 whole drawn northern pike, lake trout or substitute (3½ to 4½ lbs.), head and tail removed

6 servings

Spray cooking grate with nonstick vegetable cooking spray. Prepare grill for medium direct heat. In small mixing bowl, combine sauce ingredients. Set sauce aside. Butterfly fish as shown on page 74.

Place fish skin-side-down on prepared cooking grate. Grill, covered, for 5 minutes. Spread sauce evenly over fish. Grill, covered, for 6 to 10 minutes, or until fish is firm and opaque and just begins to flake. Garnish with snipped fresh chives and lime slices, if desired.

Per Serving: Calories: 168 • Protein: 30 g. • Carbohydrate: 5 g. • Fat: 2 g. • Cholesterol: 60 mg. • Sodium: 357 mg.
Exchanges: 4 lean meat, 1 vegetable

Bass Asarandiado

"This recipe can be applied to any large fish, especially northern pike and striped bass. We have cooked fish up to 20 lbs. in this manner, adjusting the ingredients accordingly."
Norm and Sil Strung – Bozeman, Montana

- 1 teaspoon margarine or butter
- 1 whole drawn bass or substitute (2 lbs.), scaled, head and tail removed
- 2 teaspoons fresh lime juice
- 1 teaspoon soy sauce
- ¼ teaspoon garlic salt
- ¼ cup stone-ground Dijon mustard
- ¼ cup mayonnaise

2 to 3 servings

Prepare grill for medium direct heat. Grease 14 × 14-inch sheet of heavy-duty foil with margarine. Set aside. Butterfly fish as shown on page 74.

Place fish skin-side-down on prepared foil. Fold up edges of foil to hold juices. Sprinkle fish evenly with lime juice, soy sauce and garlic salt. In small mixing bowl, combine mustard and mayonnaise. Spread mixture evenly over fish.

Place packet on cooking grate. Grill, covered, for 10 to 15 minutes, or until fish is firm and opaque and just begins to flake. Garnish with snipped fresh chives, if desired.

Per Serving: Calories: 345 • Protein: 29 g. • Carbohydrate: 4 g. • Fat: 23 g. • Cholesterol: 116 mg. • Sodium: 1092 mg.
Exchanges: 4 lean meat, ¾ vegetable, 2 fat

Spicy Marinated Salmon with Avocado Salsa

Gerard Glass – Phoenix, Arizona

MARINADE:

    1 cup vermouth
  ¾ cup olive oil
    1 tablespoon minced fresh garlic
    1 jalapeño pepper, seeded and finely chopped
        (1 tablespoon)
    1 tablespoon fresh lemon or lime juice
1½ teaspoons freshly ground pepper
    2 teaspoons red pepper sauce
1¼ teaspoons salt

    6 salmon, or substitute, steaks (8 oz. each),
        1 inch thick

SALSA:

    2 ripe avocados, peeled, seeded and finely chopped
  ¼ cup finely chopped red onion
    2 tablespoons olive oil
    2 tablespoons rice wine vinegar
    1 tablespoon snipped fresh cilantro leaves
  ¼ teaspoon salt

In 11 × 7-inch baking dish, combine marinade ingredients. Arrange steaks in single layer in baking dish, turning to coat. Cover with plastic wrap. Chill 2 hours, turning steaks over occasionally.

In medium mixing bowl, combine salsa ingredients. Cover with plastic wrap. Chill 2 hours.

Spray cooking grate with nonstick vegetable cooking spray. Prepare grill for medium direct heat. Drain and discard marinade from steaks.

Arrange steaks on prepared cooking grate. Grill, covered, for 8 to 10 minutes, or until fish is firm and opaque and just begins to flake, turning over once.

Per Serving: Calories: 400 • Protein: 26 g. • Carbohydrate: 6 g.
• Fat: 30 g. • Cholesterol: 67 mg. • Sodium: 282 mg.
Exchanges: 3 lean meat, 1¼ vegetable, 4 fat

6 servings

Brandy-barbecued Salmon Steaks

William F. Carney – Beverly, Massachusetts

MARINADE:

½ cup brandy
⅓ cup margarine or butter, melted
2 tablespoons fresh lemon juice
¼ cup snipped fresh chives
1 teaspoon soy sauce
½ teaspoon dried marjoram leaves
⅛ teaspoon salt
⅛ teaspoon freshly ground pepper

4 salmon, or substitute, steaks
    (8 oz. each), 1 inch thick

4 servings

In small mixing bowl, combine marinade ingredients. Reserve ¼ cup marinade. Cover with plastic wrap and chill. Arrange steaks in single layer in 11 × 7-inch baking dish. Pour remaining marinade over steaks, turning to coat. Cover with plastic wrap. Chill 1 ½ hours, turning steaks over occasionally.

Spray cooking grate with nonstick vegetable cooking spray. Prepare grill for medium direct heat. Drain and discard marinade from steaks. Arrange steaks on prepared cooking grate. Grill, covered, for 8 to 10 minutes, or until fish is firm and opaque and just begins to flake, basting occasionally with reserved marinade and turning over once.

Per Serving: Calories: 420 • Protein: 40 g.
• Carbohydrate: 1 g. • Fat: 22 g.
• Cholesterol: 110 mg. • Sodium: 297 mg.
Exchanges: 5¾ lean meat, 2 fat

Bluegill & Vegetable Stir-fry ↑

Mark Lisowski – Sagamore Hills, Ohio

¾ lb. sunfish, or substitute, fillets
    (2 to 3 oz. each), skin removed
1 tablespoon margarine or butter
1 medium green pepper, cut into
    ¾-inch chunks (1 cup)
1 medium onion, thinly sliced
¼ teaspoon paprika
¼ teaspoon freshly ground pepper
⅛ teaspoon salt
1 medium tomato, cut into 8 wedges

2 servings

Prepare grill for medium direct heat. Cut two 18 × 18-inch sheets of heavy-duty foil. Arrange fillets in center of 1 sheet of foil. Fold up edges of foil to hold juices. Dot fillets with margarine. Sprinkle fillets evenly with pepper chunks, onion slices, paprika, pepper and salt. Cover with remaining sheet of foil, crimping edges together to seal.

Place packet on cooking grate. Grill, covered, for 5 minutes. Stir. Re-cover. Grill for 3 minutes longer. Add tomato. Re-cover. Grill for 5 to 7 minutes, or until fish is firm and opaque and just begins to flake and tomato is hot, stirring once or twice.

Per Serving: Calories: 248 • Protein: 35 g. • Carbohydrate: 10 g. • Fat: 7 g.
• Cholesterol: 114 mg. • Sodium: 352 mg.
Exchanges: 4 lean meat, 2 vegetable

111

← Keoni's Island Broil

John P. Ko – Woodland, California

MARINADE:
½ cup soy sauce
¼ cup port wine
¼ cup water
¼ cup packed brown sugar
¼ cup sliced green onions
4 to 6 cloves garlic, minced
1 tablespoon plus 1½ teaspoons sesame oil
1 tablespoon toasted sesame seed

2 lbs. salmon, or substitute, fillets (8 oz. each), skin on

4 servings

In small mixing bowl, combine marinade ingredients. Reserve ¼ cup marinade. Cover with plastic wrap and chill. Arrange fillets in single layer in 11 × 7-inch baking dish. Pour remaining marinade over fillets, turning to coat. Cover with plastic wrap. Chill 3 hours, turning fillets over occasionally.

Spray cooking grate with nonstick vegetable cooking spray. Prepare grill for medium direct heat. Drain and discard marinade from fish. Arrange fillets on prepared cooking grate. Grill, covered, for 5 minutes. Turn fillets over. Grill for 3 to 5 minutes longer, or until fish is firm and opaque and just begins to flake, basting occasionally with reserved marinade. Serve with hot cooked rice, if desired.

Per Serving: Calories: 373 • Protein: 41 g. • Carbohydrate: 12 g. • Fat: 16 g. • Cholesterol: 110 mg. • Sodium: 1573 mg. Exchanges: 6 lean meat, ⅔ fruit

Fishwich Fillets

"A one-step meal that requires no cleanup. Ideal for camping or summer cookouts."
Norm and Sil Strung – Bozeman, Montana

2 tablespoons margarine or butter, softened
2 walleye, or substitute, fillets (1 lb. each), skin removed
½ teaspoon salt
½ teaspoon freshly ground pepper
2 cups frozen, loose-pack hash browns, divided
¼ cup barbecue sauce, divided
1 can (16 oz.) sauerkraut, rinsed and well drained, divided
1 large white onion, thinly sliced

6 servings

Prepare grill for medium direct heat. Grease center of 22 × 14-inch sheet of heavy-duty foil with margarine. Sprinkle fillets evenly with salt and pepper. Place 1 fillet on foil. Top with 1 cup hash browns, 1 tablespoon barbecue sauce, half of sauerkraut, and 1 tablespoon barbecue sauce. Arrange onion slices evenly over barbecue sauce. Top with 1 tablespoon barbecue sauce, the remaining sauerkraut, the remaining 1 tablespoon barbecue sauce and 1 cup hash browns. Place remaining fillet over hash browns.

Fold long sides of foil together in locked folds. Fold and crimp short ends; seal tightly. Leave 1-inch-long vent at top of foil packet. Place packet on cooking grate. Grill, covered, for 30 to 35 minutes, or until fish is firm and opaque and just begins to flake, hash browns are hot and onions are tender. Garnish with sliced green onions, if desired.

Per Serving: Calories: 257 • Protein: 31 g. • Carbohydrate: 18 g. • Fat: 6 g. • Cholesterol: 130 mg. • Sodium: 575 mg. Exchanges: ¾ starch, 3½ lean meat, 1¼ vegetable

Foiled Walleye Almondine

Jim Sicher – DeForest, Wisconsin

¾ lb. walleye, or substitute, fillets (6 oz. each),
  skin removed
1 tablespoon margarine or butter, softened
4 thin red onion slices
4 thin lemon slices
2 tablespoons sliced almonds
¼ cup sliced green onions
⅛ teaspoon salt
⅛ teaspoon white or lemon pepper
  Paprika

2 servings

Prepare grill for medium direct heat. Grease center of 20 × 18-inch sheet of heavy-duty foil with margarine. Arrange 2 slices each of red onion and lemon over margarine. Sprinkle with 1 tablespoon almonds and half of green onions. Arrange fillets in single layer over onions, lemon and almonds. Top with remaining red and green onions, lemon and almonds. Sprinkle lightly with salt, pepper and paprika.

Fold long sides of foil together in locked folds. Fold and crimp short ends; seal tightly. Place packet on cooking grate. Grill, covered, for 11 to 15 minutes, or until fish is firm and opaque and just begins to flake.

Per Serving: Calories: 257 • Protein: 34 g. • Carbohydrate: 5 g.
• Fat: 11 g. • Cholesterol: 146 mg. • Sodium: 294 mg.
Exchanges: 4 lean meat, 1 vegetable

Grilled Fillet of Salmon with Chives

Francois Dionot, L'Académie de Cuisine, Inc. – Bethesda, Maryland

1 salmon, or substitute, fillet (2 lbs.), skin on
2 tablespoons snipped fresh chives
1 tablespoon finely chopped shallot
½ teaspoon salt
¼ teaspoon freshly ground pepper
⅓ cup crème fraîche*

5 to 6 servings

Without cutting through skin, make diagonal crosswise cuts through fillet at 3-inch intervals. Set aside.

In small bowl, combine chives, shallot, salt and pepper. Brush crème fraîche evenly over fillet. Sprinkle evenly with chive mixture. Cover with plastic wrap. Chill 2 hours.

Spray cooking grate with nonstick vegetable cooking spray. Prepare grill for high direct heat. Place fillet skin-side-down on prepared cooking grate. Grill, covered, for 13 to 15 minutes, or until fish is firm and opaque and just begins to flake. Serve with additional crème fraîche, if desired.

* To prepare crème fraîche, combine ½ cup whipping cream and 1 tablespoon buttermilk in small mixing bowl. Cover with plastic wrap. Let stand at room temperature for 8 hours, or until mixture thickens. Store, covered, in refrigerator no longer than 2 days.

Per Serving: Calories: 262 • Protein: 30 g. • Carbohydrate: 1 g.
• Fat: 14 g. • Cholesterol: 101 mg. • Sodium: 256 mg.
Exchanges: 4¼ lean meat, ¼ fat

Herb-stuffed Barbecued Salmon

Mona L. Mundhenk – Seattle, Washington

1 tablespoon olive oil
1 medium onion, thinly sliced
3 lbs. salmon, or substitute, fillets
    (8 oz. each), skin on
3 cloves garlic, minced
1 teaspoon snipped fresh chives
1/4 teaspoon salt
1/4 teaspoon freshly ground pepper
6 thin lemon slices
1 medium tomato, thinly sliced
    (6 slices)
3 sprigs fresh dill weed
3 fresh basil leaves
3 tablespoons margarine or butter

6 servings

Prepare grill for medium direct heat. Spray one side of each of three 20 × 18-inch sheets of heavy-duty foil with nonstick vegetable cooking spray. Set aside.

In 8-inch skillet, heat oil over medium heat. Add onion. Cook for 4 to 5 minutes, or until tender, stirring frequently. Set aside.

Place 1 fillet skin-side-down in center of each sheet of prepared foil. Sprinkle evenly with garlic, chives, salt and pepper. Arrange 2 slices each of lemon and tomato on each fillet. Top evenly with onion, dill and basil. Dot evenly with margarine. Top with remaining fillets, skin-side-up.

Fold long sides of foil together in locked folds. Fold and crimp short ends; seal tightly. Arrange packets on cooking grate. Grill, covered, for 12 minutes. Turn packets over. Grill, covered, for 12 to 15 minutes longer, or until fish is firm and opaque and just begins to flake. Garnish with additional lemon and tomato slices, if desired.

Per Serving: Calories: 415 • Protein: 46 g.
• Carbohydrate: 5 g. • Fat: 23 g.
• Cholesterol: 125 mg. • Sodium: 263 mg.
Exchanges: 6 lean meat, 1 vegetable, 1 fat

Northern Beer Bites ↑

"We enjoy this recipe as an appetizer, but it may be served as a main dish."
Jim and Marianne Burke – Arlington, Texas

6 wooden skewers (10-inch)

MARINADE:
1/4 cup margarine or butter
1 tablespoon olive oil
4 to 5 cloves garlic, crushed
1/4 teaspoon instant minced onion
1/4 teaspoon snipped fresh dill weed
1/4 teaspoon salt
1/8 teaspoon freshly ground pepper
1/2 cup beer
2 northern pike, or substitute, fillets
    (12 oz. each), skin removed

4 to 6 servings

Soak wooden skewers in water for 1/2 hour. In 1-quart saucepan, combine marinade ingredients. Cook over medium-low heat for 3 to 5 minutes, or until margarine is melted and mixture is hot, stirring occasionally. Remove from heat. Blend in beer. Set aside.

Cut each fillet lengthwise into three 10 × 1-inch strips. Thread 1 strip on each skewer, accordion-style. Arrange skewers in single layer in 11 × 7-inch baking dish. Pour marinade mixture over fish, turning skewers to coat. Cover with plastic wrap. Refrigerate 8 hours or overnight, turning over occasionally.

Spray cooking grate with nonstick vegetable cooking spray. Prepare grill for medium direct heat. Drain and discard marinade from fish. Arrange skewers on prepared cooking grate. Grill, covered, for 3 minutes. Turn skewers over. Grill, covered, for 2 to 3 minutes longer, or until fish is firm and opaque and just begins to flake. Serve with drawn butter and lemon wedges, if desired.

Per Serving: Calories: 151 • Protein: 22 g. • Carbohydrate: 1 g. • Fat: 6 g.
• Cholesterol: 44 mg. • Sodium: 137 mg.
Exchanges: 3 lean meat

Reed's Cajun Baked Salmon →

"This recipe has a little kick, but it won't burn your mouth. For those who like things really hot, add a few hot peppers while it's baking, but remove them before serving."
  Reed J. Huenink – West Allis, Wisconsin

SEASONING:
1¼ teaspoons garlic powder
1¼ teaspoons freshly ground pepper
  1 teaspoon seasoned salt
  ½ teaspoon white pepper
  ½ teaspoon cayenne
  ½ teaspoon onion powder
  ¼ teaspoon paprika
  ¼ teaspoon dried parsley flakes

  1 salmon, or substitute, fillet (2 lbs.), skin on
  1 large onion, thinly sliced
1½ cups sliced black olives
  1 cup shredded mozzarella cheese

5 to 6 servings

Prepare grill for medium direct heat. In small mixing bowl, combine seasoning ingredients. Place fillet skin-side-down on 24 × 18-inch sheet of heavy-duty foil. Sprinkle evenly with seasoning mixture. Layer onion, olives and cheese evenly over fillet.

Fold long sides of foil together in locked folds. Fold and crimp short ends; seal tightly. Place packet on cooking grate. Grill, covered, for 20 to 28 minutes, or until fish is firm and opaque and just begins to flake.

Per Serving: Calories: 314 • Protein: 34 g. • Carbohydrate: 5 g. • Fat: 17 g. • Cholesterol: 98 mg. • Sodium: 579 mg.
Exchanges: 4½ lean meat, 1 vegetable, ½ fat

Catfish Mexicana

"I like my sauce on the hot side, so I add hot taco sauce."
William E. Pugh – Cleveland, Ohio

  ½ cup milk
  ½ teaspoon ground cumin
1 ½ lbs. catfish fillets (6 oz. each),
       skin removed
  2 tablespoons olive oil
  1 medium onion, finely chopped
       (1 cup)
  ½ cup chopped green, red or
       yellow pepper
  ¼ cup snipped fresh cilantro leaves
  ¼ teaspoon salt
  ¼ teaspoon freshly ground pepper
  4 teaspoons taco sauce or salsa
       (optional)

4 servings

Combine milk and cumin in large, sealable plastic food-storage bag. Add fillets, turning to coat. Seal bag. Chill 1 hour.

In 8-inch skillet, heat oil over medium heat. Add onion. Cook for 2 to 3 minutes, or until onion is tender. Reduce heat to low. Stir in chopped pepper, cilantro, salt and pepper. Simmer, uncovered, for 1 to 2 minutes, or until chopped pepper is tender-crisp. Set aside.

Prepare grill for high direct heat. Drain and discard milk mixture from fish. Cut four 14 × 12-inch sheets of heavy-duty foil. Place 1 fillet on each sheet of foil. Top each fillet with one-fourth of vegetable mixture and 1 teaspoon taco sauce. Fold long sides of foil together in locked folds. Fold and crimp short ends; seal tightly.

Place packets on cooking grate. Grill, covered, for 11 to 17 minutes, or until fish is firm and opaque and just begins to flake. Garnish with lemon and lime wedges, if desired.

Per Serving: Calories: 290 • Protein: 33 g.
• Carbohydrate: 5 g. • Fat: 15 g.
• Cholesterol: 101 mg. • Sodium: 259 mg.
Exchanges: 4 lean meat, 1 vegetable, ½ fat

Lake Trout à la Larsen

"The secret tip is soaking the fish in milk overnight. My recipe is very simple and very tasty."
Bob Larsen – Chicago, Illinois

2¼ lbs. lake trout, or substitute, fillets
       (6 oz. each), skin removed
2½ cups milk
  4 cloves garlic, thinly sliced
  1 small lemon, thinly sliced, divided

  8 oz. fresh mushrooms, sliced
       (2 cups)
  1 cup diagonally sliced green
       onions
  1 cup dry white wine

6 servings

Arrange fillets in single layer in 11 × 7-inch baking dish. Pour milk over fillets. Cover with plastic wrap. Refrigerate overnight.

Prepare grill for medium direct heat. Drain and discard milk from fillets. Rinse and pat dry. Make 14 × 9 × 2-inch pan from 2 layered sheets of heavy-duty foil. Arrange fillets in pan. Sprinkle with garlic, half of lemon slices, the mushrooms and onions.

Place pan on cooking grate. Pour wine over fillets and vegetables. Grill, covered, for 15 to 20 minutes, or until vegetables are tender and fish is firm and opaque and just begins to flake. Garnish with remaining lemon.

Per Serving: Calories: 304 • Protein: 37 g. • Carbohydrate: 6 g. • Fat: 12 g.
• Cholesterol: 99 mg. • Sodium: 99 mg.
Exchanges: 5 lean meat, 1 vegetable

Gingered Catfish Fillets

Jude W. Theriot – Lake Charles, Louisiana

¼ cup margarine or butter
¼ cup peanut oil
¼ cup reduced-sodium soy sauce
2 tablespoons butter-flavored granules
2 teaspoons white wine Worcestershire sauce
2 teaspoons tarragon vinegar
2 teaspoons grated fresh gingerroot
½ teaspoon red pepper sauce
½ teaspoon white pepper
¼ to ½ teaspoon crushed red pepper flakes (optional)
2¼ lbs. catfish fillets (6 oz. each), skin removed

6 servings

In 1-quart saucepan, combine all ingredients, except fillets. Simmer over low heat for 3 to 5 minutes, or until mixture thickens slightly. Remove from heat. Set marinade aside to cool completely. Reserve ½ cup marinade. Cover with plastic wrap. Chill.

Arrange fillets in single layer in 11 × 7-inch baking dish. Pour remaining marinade over fillets. Cover with plastic wrap. Chill 2 hours, turning fillets over once.

Spray cooking grate with nonstick vegetable cooking spray. Prepare grill for high direct heat. Drain and discard marinade from fish. Arrange fillets on prepared cooking grate. Baste with reserved marinade. Grill for 3 minutes. Turn fillets over. Grill for 3 to 5 minutes longer, or until fish is firm and opaque and just begins to flake, basting frequently with reserved marinade.

Per Serving: Calories: 321 • Protein: 31 g. • Carbohydrate: 1 g. • Fat: 21 g. • Cholesterol: 99 mg. • Sodium: 627 mg. Exchanges: 4½ lean meat, ¼ vegetable, 1½ fat

Grilled Marinated Frog Legs ↑

Keith Sutton – Benton, Arkansas

6 pairs frog legs (about 2 lbs.), skin removed

MARINADE:
½ cup vegetable oil
3 tablespoons finely chopped red onion
2 tablespoons snipped fresh parsley
1 tablespoon grated lemon peel
1 tablespoon plus 1½ teaspoons lemon juice
1 teaspoon salt
1 teaspoon dry mustard
1 teaspoon dried basil leaves
¼ cup margarine or butter
1 clove garlic, minced

3 to 6 servings

Arrange frog legs in single layer in 11 × 7-inch baking dish. In small mixing bowl, combine marinade ingredients. Reserve ⅓ cup marinade. Cover with plastic wrap. Chill. Pour remaining marinade over frog legs, turning to coat. Cover with plastic wrap. Chill 3 hours, turning legs over occasionally.

Spray cooking grate with nonstick vegetable cooking spray. Prepare grill for medium direct heat. Drain and discard marinade from frog legs. Arrange legs on prepared cooking grate. Grill, covered, for 3 minutes. Turn legs over. Grill, covered, for 3 to 5 minutes longer, or until meat is no longer pink and begins to pull away from bone.

In 1-quart saucepan, combine reserved marinade with margarine and garlic. Cook over medium heat for 1 to 2 minutes, or until mixture is hot and margarine is melted, stirring frequently. Before serving, pour margarine mixture over frog legs.

Per Serving: Calories: 206 • Protein: 16 g. • Carbohydrate: 1 g. • Fat: 15 g. • Cholesterol: 49 mg. • Sodium: 422 mg. Exchanges: 2¼ lean meat, ¼ vegetable, 1½ fat

117

Campfire Cooking

Techniques for Campfire Cooking

EQUIPMENT for campfire cooking includes (1) grate; (2) long-handled spatula, (3) long-handled fork or (4) tongs for handling fish; (5) oven mitt; (6) cooking oil; (7) wooden matches in a waterproof container; (8) newspaper for starting fire; (9) seasoned cast-iron frying pan and (10) heavy-duty aluminum foil, for wrapping fish and to prevent sticking.

When you've worked up an appetite from a long morning of fishing, a "shore lunch" cooked over a campfire makes an unforgettable treat. The traditional shore lunch consists of fried fish, potatoes and a can of baked beans, but practically anything you cook tastes great in the fresh air.

Build a fire using dry, nonresinous hardwoods, preferably logs about 3 to 4 inches in diameter and some smaller kindling. If it has been raining, you may have to carry some newspaper or dry tinder to get the fire started. Stack the wood in log-cabin or teepee style over the tinder.

When the fire has burned down to a bed of hot coals, place a grate over coals on rocks or logs bordering the fire. Feed the fire with small twigs as needed to maintain even heat.

The usual way to cook over a campfire is simply to set a frying pan on the grate. But you can also wrap the fish in a foil packet, along with vegetables, if desired, and set the packet directly on the coals.

When you're done cooking, be sure to extinguish your fire by covering it with dirt or sand.

How to Cook Fish in a Frying Pan

TEST the coals by blowing on them; when they glow bright red, the fire is ready. Don't attempt to cook until the flames disappear.

PLACE rocks around the fire to hold the grate about 4 to 8 inches above the coals. Lower the height of the grate for more heat or raise it for less heat.

ADD 2 or 3 tablespoons of cooking oil to the frying pan and heat for 1 to 2 minutes. Use long-handled tongs or fork to add the fish.

How to Cook Fish in Coals

DOUBLE-WRAP fish by first criss-crossing two sheets of heavy-duty aluminum foil. Wrap fish in top sheet as shown; repeat with bottom sheet.

SET the foil package in the middle of the coals. Cooking time will vary depending on weather, size of package and intensity of heat.

COOK for half the recommended time. Using long-handled tongs, turn package over and cook for remaining time. Open package to test doneness.

Tips for Campfire Cooking

HOLD your hand 6 to 8 inches above grate to judge heat. If you can hold it there 2 to 4 seconds, the heat is high; 5 to 7 seconds, medium; 8 to 10 seconds, low.

PREMIX flour or desired coating with dried herbs and other seasonings in a resealable plastic bag. To coat fish pieces, add them to the bag, reseal and shake.

KEEP the spice mixture needed for your recipe in a 35 mm film cannister. This way, you'll be sure to have the proper blend and you won't have to carry several bottles.

CARRY a small cooler for perishable foods and supplies such as cooking oil, matches, newspaper, seasonings and utensils. Water frozen in plastic bottles keeps food cool.

← Salsa-stuffed Trout

"This recipe is extremely easy to make and very healthy. You can prepare the salsa beforehand when camping by putting it in a sealable plastic bag and keeping it cool. We find that the salsa gives the fish a subtle, clean flavor."
Michael R. Lehnert – Battle Ground, Washington

1	whole drawn lake trout or substitute (1½ to 2 lbs.), head removed
3	Roma tomatoes, seeded and chopped (¾ cup)
⅓	cup sliced green onions
½	cup thinly sliced celery
⅓	cup snipped fresh parsley
3	tablespoons snipped fresh cilantro leaves
1	jalapeño pepper, seeded and minced (2 tablespoons)
1	tablespoon snipped fresh basil leaves
1	teaspoon salt
½	teaspoon white pepper

3 to 4 servings

Build a campfire and allow it to burn down to glowing coals. Cut two 30 × 18-inch sheets of heavy-duty foil. Place trout in center of 1 sheet. In medium mixing bowl, combine remaining ingredients. Stuff cavity of fish with vegetable mixture, spreading any excess mixture on top of fish.

Fold long sides of foil together in locked folds. Fold and crimp short ends; seal tightly. Place packet seam-side-down on second sheet of foil. Fold as directed above. Place packet on cooking grate over campfire. Cook for 10 minutes. Turn packet over. Cook for 5 to 10 minutes longer, or until fish begins to flake when fork is inserted at backbone in thickest part of fish.

Per Serving: Calories: 238 • Protein: 32 g. • Carbohydrate: 4 g. • Fat: 10 g. • Cholesterol: 87 mg. • Sodium: 647 mg. Exchanges: 4 lean meat, ½ vegetable

Frances's Campfire Trout

Frances D. Squier – Aberdeen, North Carolina

2	whole drawn stream trout (8 oz. each)
1	small onion, cut into 6 wedges
2	tablespoons snipped fresh sorrel or wild dock leaves
2	teaspoons margarine or butter
¼	teaspoon salt
¼	teaspoon pepper
4	to 6 large fresh sorrel, wild dock or Bibb lettuce leaves

2 servings

Build a campfire and allow it to burn down to glowing coals. Cut two 18 × 14-inch sheets of heavy-duty foil. Place 1 trout in center of each sheet. Stuff each fish evenly with onion, snipped sorrel and margarine. Sprinkle cavity of each fish evenly with salt and pepper. Wrap body of each fish with sorrel leaves, leaving head and tail exposed.

Fold long sides of foil together in locked folds. Fold and crimp short ends; seal tightly. Place packets directly on coals. Cook for 4 minutes. Turn packets over. Cook for 4 to 6 minutes longer, or until fish begins to flake when fork is inserted at backbone in thickest part of fish.

Per Serving: Calories: 210 • Protein: 29 g. • Carbohydrate: 4 g. • Fat: 8 g. • Cholesterol: 76 mg. • Sodium: 353 mg. Exchanges: 4 lean meat, ½ vegetable

Lemony Apple-stuffed Salmon ↑

"This family recipe has never been written down before."
Kevin and Denise Greve – Goshen, Kentucky

1 whole drawn salmon or substitute (2½ to 3 lbs.), head removed
1 teaspoon dried dill weed
1 medium red cooking apple, cored and cut into thin wedges
½ medium onion, thinly sliced
4 thin lemon slices
½ cup margarine or butter, melted

4 servings

Build a campfire and allow it to burn down to glowing coals. Cut two 36 × 18-inch sheets of heavy-duty foil. Place salmon in center of 1 sheet. Turn up edges slightly. Sprinkle cavity of fish with dill. Stuff cavity of fish with apple, onion and lemon slices. Brush fish lightly with margarine. Pour remaining margarine over stuffing.

Fold long sides of foil together in locked folds. Fold and crimp short ends; seal tightly. Place packet seam-side-down on second sheet of foil. Fold as directed above. Place packet on cooking grate over campfire. Cook for 15 minutes. Turn packet over. Cook for 15 to 20 minutes longer, or until fish begins to flake when fork is inserted at backbone in thickest part of fish.

Per Serving: Calories: 492 • Protein: 37 g. • Carbohydrate: 7 g. • Fat: 35 g. • Cholesterol: 102 mg. • Sodium: 350 mg. Exchanges: 3 lean meat, ⅓ fruit, 2½ fat

Riverside Bullheads

Keith Sutton – Benton, Arkansas

1 tablespoon margarine or butter, softened
6 whole drawn bullheads (4 to 6 oz. each), skin and heads removed
8 oz. fresh mushrooms, sliced (2 cups)
⅔ cup dry white wine
¼ cup chopped onion
2 tablespoons vegetable oil
1 tablespoon plus 1½ teaspoons dried parsley flakes
1 tablespoon plus 1½ teaspoons fresh lemon juice
¼ teaspoon salt
¼ teaspoon freshly ground pepper
¼ teaspoon dried thyme leaves

3 servings

Build a campfire and allow it to burn down to glowing coals. Cut six 18 × 14-inch sheets of heavy-duty foil. Spread ½ teaspoon margarine on each sheet of foil. Place 1 bullhead in center of each sheet. Turn up edges slightly. In medium mixing bowl, combine remaining ingredients. Spread heaping ⅓ cup of mixture evenly over each fish.

Fold long sides of foil together in locked folds. Fold and crimp short ends; seal tightly. Place packets on cooking grate over campfire. Cook for 9 minutes. Turn packets over. Cook for 5 to 9 minutes longer, or until fish begins to flake when fork is inserted at backbone in thickest part of fish.

Per Serving: Calories: 288 • Protein: 20 g. • Carbohydrate: 5 g. • Fat: 17 g. • Cholesterol: 57 mg. • Sodium: 293 mg. Exchanges: 3 lean meat, 1 vegetable, ¼ fruit, 1¾ fat

Steak à la Woodsman

Don Carpenter – Annapolis, Maryland

> 2 salmon, or substitute, steaks (8 oz. each), 1 inch thick
> 1½ teaspoons salt
> 3 tablespoons margarine or butter

2 servings

Build a campfire and allow it to burn down to glowing coals. Remove all moisture from surface of steaks by blotting with paper towels. Set aside.

Sprinkle salt in even layer over bottom of 8-inch cast-iron skillet. Place skillet on cooking grate over campfire. When drop of water flicked onto skillet dances across it, squarely drop steaks into skillet. Sear steaks for 10 seconds on each side. Add margarine to skillet. Cook for 4 minutes. Turn steaks over. Cook for 4 to 6 minutes longer, or until fish is firm and opaque and just begins to flake.

Per Serving: Calories: 436 • Protein: 40 g. • Carbohydrate: 1 g. • Fat: 30 g. • Cholesterol: 110 mg. • Sodium: 1936 mg. Exchanges: 5 lean meat, 3 fat

Layered Fish & Vegetable Bake

Yvonne Blasko – Savanna, Illinois

> 2 tablespoons margarine or butter
> 1 medium onion, thinly sliced
> 1 medium tomato, thinly sliced
> 2 medium red potatoes, thinly sliced
> 1½ lbs. walleye, salmon, or substitute, fillets (6 oz. each), skin removed
> 2 cups fresh broccoli flowerets
> 2 tablespoons fresh lemon juice
> 1 clove garlic, minced
> ¼ teaspoon salt
> ¼ teaspoon freshly ground pepper

4 servings

Build a campfire and allow it to burn down to glowing coals. Dot 11 × 9 × 1-inch foil pan with margarine. Layer onion, tomato, potatoes, fillets and broccoli in pan. Sprinkle lemon juice, garlic, salt and pepper evenly over broccoli.

Cover pan with heavy-duty foil. Place pan on cooking grate over campfire. Cook for 12 to 15 minutes, or until fish is firm and opaque and just begins to flake, and vegetables are tender-crisp.

Per Serving: Calories: 308 • Protein: 37 g. • Carbohydrate: 22 g. • Fat: 8 g. • Cholesterol: 146 mg. • Sodium: 313 mg. Exchanges: ¾ starch, 4 lean meat, 2 vegetable

Campfire Catfish

"This is a favorite family recipe."
Russell L. Allen – Freeport, Illinois

SEASONING MIX:

- 1/4 teaspoon seasoned salt
- 1/4 teaspoon pepper
- 1/4 teaspoon garlic powder
- 1/4 teaspoon ground nutmeg

- 1 1/2 lbs. catfish, walleye, or substitute, fillets (6 oz. each), skin removed
- 1/4 cup diagonally sliced green onions
- 1/2 medium green pepper, finely chopped
- 1 jar (2 oz.) diced pimiento, drained
- 2 tablespoons margarine or butter

4 servings

Build a campfire and allow it to burn down to glowing coals. In small bowl, combine seasoning mix ingredients. Set aside. Cut four 18 × 14-inch sheets of heavy-duty foil. Place 2 fillets in center of each of 2 sheets of foil. Sprinkle fillets evenly with seasoning mix, onions, green pepper and pimiento. Dot evenly with margarine.

Fold long sides of foil together in locked folds. Fold and crimp short ends; seal tightly. Place packets seam-side-down on remaining 2 sheets of foil. Fold as directed above. Place packets directly on coals. Cook for 5 minutes. Turn packets over. Cook for 3 to 5 minutes longer, or until fish is firm and opaque and just begins to flake.

Per Serving: Calories: 258 • Protein: 31 g.
• Carbohydrate: 2 g. • Fat: 13 g.
• Cholesterol: 99 mg. • Sodium: 253 mg.
Exchanges: 4 lean meat, 1/2 vegetable

Salmon aux Pommes ↑

"This recipe may be used with any fillet, but is especially adapted to the chinook salmon. It is an Alaskan guide streamside recipe."
Arthur Davenport – Belchertown, Massachusetts

- 1 1/2 lbs. salmon, or substitute, fillets (6 oz. each), skin removed
- 2 teaspoons lemon pepper
- 2 teaspoons fresh lemon juice
- 1 medium red cooking apple, cored and cut into 12 wedges
- 1 medium green cooking apple, cored and cut into 12 wedges

4 servings

Build a campfire and allow it to burn down to glowing coals. Cut eight 14 × 14-inch sheets of heavy-duty foil. Place 1 fillet in center of each of 4 sheets of foil. Sprinkle evenly with lemon pepper and juice. Arrange 3 red and 3 green apple wedges over each fillet.

Fold opposite sides of foil together in locked folds. Fold and crimp remaining sides; seal tightly. Place packets seam-side-down on remaining 4 sheets of foil. Fold as directed above. Place packets on cooking grate over campfire. Cook for 10 minutes. Turn packets over. Cook for 10 to 12 minutes longer, or until fish is firm and opaque and just begins to flake.

Per Serving: Calories: 286 • Protein: 34 g. • Carbohydrate: 11 g. • Fat: 11 g.
• Cholesterol: 94 mg. • Sodium: 478 mg.
Exchanges: 4 lean meat, 3/4 fruit

Blackened Fish

"You can make your Cajun seasoning hotter or milder by adjusting the amount of pepper."
Clif and Betty Santa – Vermilion Bay, Ontario

CAJUN SEASONING:

1 tablespoon paprika
2½ teaspoons salt
1 teaspoon onion powder
1 teaspoon garlic powder
1 teaspoon cayenne
¾ teaspoon white pepper
¾ teaspoon black pepper
½ teaspoon dried thyme leaves, crushed
½ teaspoon dried oregano leaves

2¼ lbs. catfish, lake trout, or substitute, fillets
(6 oz. each), skin removed, cut in half crosswise

6 servings

Build a campfire and allow it to burn down to glowing coals. In shallow bowl, combine seasoning ingredients. Set aside. Place cast-iron skillet on cooking grate over campfire. When drop of water flicked onto skillet dances across it, skillet is hot. Dredge both sides of each fillet in seasoning mixture.

Squarely drop fillets into skillet. Cook for 2 minutes on each side, or until fish is firm and opaque and just begins to flake.

Per Serving: Calories: 261 • Protein: 36 g. • Carbohydrate: 2 g. • Fat: 11 g. • Cholesterol: 99 mg. • Sodium: 1005 mg.
Exchanges: 5 lean meat

Hot Waldorf Crayfish ↑

Thomas K. Squier – Aberdeen, North Carolina

1 lb. cooked crayfish tails, in shell
2 medium red or green cooking apples, each cored and cut into 8 wedges
½ cup chopped pecans or walnuts
¼ cup margarine or butter

2 servings

Build a campfire and allow it to burn down to glowing coals. Cut four 18 × 14-inch sheets of heavy-duty foil. Place half of crayfish tails in center of each of 2 sheets of foil. Top each with half of apple wedges and pecans. Dot evenly with margarine.

Fold long sides of foil together in locked folds. Fold and crimp short ends; seal tightly. Place packets seam-side-down on remaining 2 sheets of foil. Fold as directed above. Place packets directly on coals. Cook for 4 minutes. Turn packets over. Cook for 3 to 5 minutes longer, or until apples are tender-crisp and mixture is hot.

Per Serving: Calories: 639 • Protein: 39 g. • Carbohydrate: 26 g. • Fat: 44 g. • Cholesterol: 271 mg. • Sodium: 371 mg.
Exchanges: 5 lean meat, 1½ fruit, 5¾ fat

Trout Cakes with Celery Sauce

Albia Dugger – Miami, Florida

- 2 tablespoons margarine or butter
- 1 medium onion, finely chopped
- 1 small red pepper, seeded and finely chopped
- 1 cup water
- 1 teaspoon instant chicken bouillon granules
- ½ teaspoon Worcestershire sauce
- ½ teaspoon red pepper sauce
- ½ teaspoon freshly ground pepper
- 1 lb. stream trout, or substitute, fillets
- 1 teaspoon fresh lemon juice
- 1 can (10¾ oz.) condensed cream of celery soup, divided
- 2 cups instant potato buds or flakes
- ½ cup seasoned dry bread crumbs
- 6 tablespoons vegetable oil
- 12 slices (¾ oz. each) pasteurized process American cheese (optional)
- ¼ cup evaporated milk

6 servings

Per Serving: Calories: 411 • Protein: 20 g. • Carbohydrate: 30 g.
• Fat: 24 g. • Cholesterol: 52 mg. • Sodium: 929 mg.
Exchanges: 1¾ starch, 2 lean meat, ½ vegetable, 3½ fat

How to Prepare Trout Cakes with Celery Sauce

BUILD campfire; allow to burn down to glowing coals. Place 10-inch cast-iron skillet on grate over coals. Melt margarine in skillet. Add onion and red pepper. Cook for 1 to 2 minutes.

ADD water, bouillon, Worcestershire sauce, red pepper sauce and pepper. Cook for 1 to 2 minutes. Add trout fillets. Cook for 3 to 5 minutes, or until fish is firm and completely flaked.

REMOVE skillet from cooking grate. Add lemon juice and ⅓ can of soup (about ⅓ cup). Gradually stir in potato flakes until mixture is stiff. Let cool for 5 minutes.

PLACE bread crumbs on plate. Divide fish mixture into 12 portions. Shape each into 3½-inch patty. Dredge both sides of each patty in bread crumbs. Wipe out skillet. Place on cooking grate. Heat 2 tablespoons oil.

ADD 4 patties. Cook for 4 to 6 minutes, or until golden brown, turning once and topping with cheese during final minutes of cooking time. Place on plate. Cover to keep warm. Repeat with remaining oil, patties and cheese.

WIPE out skillet. Add remaining soup and the evaporated milk. Cook mixture for 5 to 6 minutes, or until hot, stirring constantly. Spoon about 1 tablespoon sauce over each cake.

Smoke Cooking

Techniques for Smoke Cooking

Home-smoked fish makes a mouth-watering appetizer and adds a distinctive flavor to casseroles and other main dishes.

The two basic smoking methods are cold smoking and hot smoking. Cold smoking, done mainly by commercial processors, preserves the fish so it can be kept as long as 3 months. Cold-smoked fish are not cooked, they're cured. The internal temperature never exceeds 100°F during the smoking process, which may take a week or more. Hot smoking, also called smoke cooking, is easily done at home and is the method used for the recipes in this book. Hot-smoked fish are heated to at least 180°F. They're much more perishable than cold-smoked fish, but can be kept as long as 2 weeks if loosely wrapped and refrigerated.

Virtually any kind of fish can be smoked, but oily fish (p. 6) are best. They absorb the smoke better than lean fish and aren't as likely to dry out during the smoking process. Skin-on fillets or steaks, no more than 1 inch thick, are easiest to smoke, but thicker pieces or whole fish may also be used.

ELECTRIC SMOKERS are the most popular type. A pan of hardwood chips rests on a burner at the bottom, and the fish are placed on removable wire racks. These smokers are convenient and are available in several sizes, but they don't work well in cold weather.

KETTLE GRILLS double as smokers, although their capacity is limited. Simply put a small pile of charcoal briquets on the bottom and spread them when they're hot. Add a few hardwood sticks and place the fish on the grate. Control the heat by adjusting the air vents.

130

Either fresh or defrosted frozen fish can be smoked. You can also smoke fish and then freeze it, but when defrosted, the meat tends to be watery.

BRINING. Before smoking, the fish must be soaked in a salt solution, or *brine*, to kill any microorganisms.

Brining times vary from 6 to 24 hours, depending mainly on size of the pieces; the normal range is 8 to 12 hours. Some species, however, absorb the brine more quickly than others, and defrosted fish take the brine more rapidly than fresh ones, so you may have to experiment to attain the degree of saltiness that suits your taste. You can reduce brining time by using a concentrated brine.

TYPES OF SMOKERS. Hot smoking may be done in practically any kind of enclosure in which the air flow can be regulated. A variety of commonly used smokers is shown here.

The heat source may be an electric or gas burner, or just a pile of charcoal briquets. In most cases, a pan of hardwood chips or sawdust is placed on the heat source and air vents are used to regulate the temperature.

Most smoking is done with dry heat, but water smokers are gaining in popularity. A pan of water placed above the wood chips produces steam that helps keep the fish moist while it smokes. Water smokers cook the fish in about half as much time as dry smokers. However, water smoking does not preserve the fish, so it should be kept refrigerated and eaten within a few days.

OLD STOVES, especially gas models, make ideal smokers. They're insulated, have heat-resistant racks and usually require no extra venting. Just remove the broiler rack, put a pan of charcoal briquets or a large electric burner in the broiler compartment, and add a few hardwood sticks or a pan of shavings. Drill a hole in the top for a thermometer.

STEEL GARBAGE CANS, preferably new ones, easily convert to smokers. Drill holes in the sides and insert metal rods to support grates. Set a burner on the bottom, cut a hole large enough for a frying pan and save the metal to make a closing flap. Cut vent holes in the lid.

WATER SMOKERS have a heat source, either gas or electric, at the bottom and an extra grate below the fish for holding a pan of water. The steam keeps the fish moist and, if you substitute wine or other flavored liquids for the water, imparts a unique flavor to fish.

131

Wood Selection Chart

MATERIAL	FLAVOR		
	Mild	Medium	Strong
Cherry		X	
Apple		X	
Plum		X	
Pear		X	
Hickory			X
Almond		X	
Maple		X	
Alder	X		
Mesquite			X
Raspberry		X	
Grape Vine		X	
Corn Cobs	X		

FORMS OF WOOD FOR SMOKING include (1) sawdust and (2) wood chips, used mainly with a pan placed on an electric or gas burner. On an exposed bed of charcoal, use (3) sticks $1/2$ to $3/4$ inch in diameter.

Tips for Smoking Fish

SOAK wood chips to make them burn more slowly. The chips should smolder, rather than burst into flames.

ADD wine or flavorings such as stick cinnamon or lemon juice to the water pan when wet smoking, to flavor the fish.

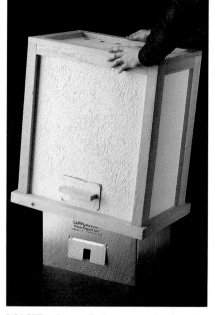

MAKE a loose-fitting cover from ceiling tiles and 1×2 strips of wood to hold the heat in an electric smoker when smoking in cold weather.

How to Smoke Fish

1. BRINE the fish in a solution of canning or pickling salt and water (see recipes for specific amounts). One gallon will brine 5 pounds of fish. Cover bowl with plastic wrap and refrigerate at 40°F for the recommended time.

2. AIR DRY the fish on a wire rack after patting it dry with paper towels. A shiny film, called a *pellicle*, will form in about an hour; this helps seal in juices. You can use a fan to form the pellicle faster.

3. PREHEAT the smoker to 100°F, checking the temperature with an oven thermometer. In cold or windy weather, you may have to put an insulating cover over the smoker (opposite page) to maintain the desired temperature.

4. PLACE fillets (skin side down) or steaks on greased racks. The racks may have to be rotated during the smoking process; fish on the bottom rack tend to cook more quickly. There is no need to turn the fish over on the racks.

5. PLACE a pan of hardwood chips on the burner, put the cover on the smoker and allow the fish to smoke. The air temperature inside the smoker should reach about 225°F. Add more chips as needed for desired flavor.

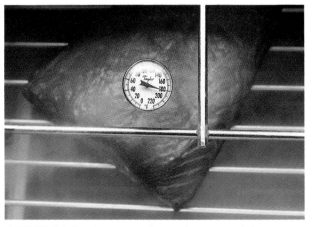

6. TEST fish for doneness using an instant-read thermometer. When the internal temperature of the fish reaches 180°F, try to maintain that temperature for an additional 30 minutes before removing from smoker.

Alder-smoked Trout

"Smoking your fillets on the charcoal grill is simple. Get ready for the finest smoked fish you've ever eaten."

Clif and Betty Santa – Vermilion Bay, Ontario

2 lake trout, or substitute, fillets (1½ lbs. each), 1 inch thick, skin on

2 tablespoons canning or pickling salt

½ teaspoon liquid smoke flavoring

1 cup packed brown sugar
Green alder wood branches (finger and thumb-size in diameter and short enough to fit inside charcoal grill)

12 servings

Place fillets skin-side-down in 13 × 9-inch baking dish. Sprinkle evenly with salt and liquid smoke. Sprinkle with sugar. Cover dish with plastic wrap. Refrigerate 24 hours, turning fillets over after 6 hours. (After about 6 hours, salt, liquid smoke and sugar create thick, dark syrup.)

Next day, remove bottom grate from charcoal grill. Light coals in bottom of grill. When coals are well lit, spread them evenly in single layer over bottom of grill. Layer branches directly over coals, stacking 3 to 4 inches deep. Spray cooking grate with nonstick vegetable cooking spray. Place prepared grate on top of branches.

Arrange fillets skin-side-down on grate. Place oven thermometer on grate next to fillets. Cover grill. Close 2 of 3 bottom drafts on grill. After 10 minutes, temperature should register about 155°F. (If too hot, close vent on grill cover.)

Smoke fillets for 2 hours, or until fish is firm and opaque and internal temperature registers 180°F in thickest part of fillets, checking grill temperature every 20 minutes. Remove fillets from grill. Chill. Serve with thick slices of crusty French bread or crackers.

Per Serving: Calories: 219 • Protein: 24 g.
• Carbohydrate: 13 g. • Fat: 8 g.
• Cholesterol: 66 mg. • Sodium: 892 mg.
Exchanges: 3½ lean meat, ¾ fruit

Smoked Carp Ribs

"Not only do they taste great, the built-in 'toothpick' makes them easy to eat."
Jim Schneider – New Ulm, Minnesota

1 whole drawn carp (12 lbs.), head removed

8 cups water

½ cup canning or pickling salt

1 small onion, thinly sliced

4 to 6 servings

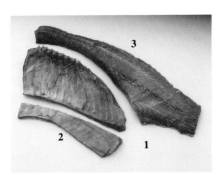

FILLET the fish, but do not remove the skin; cut off (1) rib section (approximately 1 lb.) and remove (2) belly meat. Rinse well. Reserve the (3) rest of the meat for future use.

In 5-quart glass or plastic container, combine water and salt. Stir until salt is dissolved. Add ribs to brine. Cover and refrigerate 12 hours or overnight.

Drain and discard brine from ribs. Rinse with water. Pat dry with paper towels. Arrange ribs on cooling racks.

Spread onion slices evenly over each rib portion. Air dry for 1 hour, or until ribs are shiny and dry.

Place oven thermometer in smoker. Heat dry smoker for 20 minutes, or until temperature registers 100°F. Spray smoker racks with nonstick vegetable cooking spray. Arrange ribs on prepared racks, spacing at least ½ inch apart.

Smoke ribs according to smoker manufacturer's directions (approximately 4 to 6 hours), or until fish is firm and opaque and internal temperature registers 180°F in thickest part of ribs, adding wood chips as necessary to impart desired flavor and to maintain desired level of smoke. Cut between individual ribs to make serving-size pieces. Store smoked fish, loosely wrapped, in refrigerator no longer than 2 weeks.

Nutritional information not available.

Smoked Bullheads

Jim Schneider – New Ulm, Minnesota

8 cups water
¾ cup canning or pickling salt

3 lbs. whole drawn bullheads (4 to
   6 oz. each), heads removed

6 servings

In 5-quart glass or plastic container, combine water and salt. Stir until salt is dissolved. Set aside. Remove tails, fins, spine and belly meat from bullheads. Rinse well. Add fish to brine. Cover and refrigerate 12 hours or overnight.

Drain and discard brine from fish. Rinse with water. Pat dry with paper towels. Arrange fish on cooling racks. Air dry for 1 hour, or until fish are shiny and dry.

Place oven thermometer in smoker. Heat dry smoker for 20 minutes, or until temperature registers 100°F. Spray smoker racks with nonstick vegetable cooking spray. Arrange fish, belly-side-down, on prepared racks, spacing at least ½ inch apart.

Smoke fish according to smoker manufacturer's directions (approximately 4 to 6 hours), or until fish is firm and opaque and internal temperature registers 180°F in thickest part of fish, adding wood chips as necessary to impart desired flavor and to maintain desired level of smoke. Store smoked fish, loosely wrapped, in refrigerator no longer than 2 weeks. Serve with crackers.

Per Serving: Calories: 108 • Protein: 17 g. • Carbohydrate: 0 • Fat: 4 g.
• Cholesterol: 54 mg. • Sodium: 728 mg.
Exchanges: 2 lean meat

← Smoked Salmon

Ron Cotterman – Eagle River, Alaska

BRINE:

3 cups water
3 cups dry white wine
2 cups soy sauce
1⅔ cups sugar
½ cup canning or pickling salt
½ teaspoon garlic powder
½ teaspoon onion powder
½ teaspoon pepper
½ teaspoon red pepper sauce

8 salmon, or substitute, steaks
   (8 oz. each), 1 inch thick

16 servings

In 5-quart glass or plastic container, combine brine ingredients. Stir until sugar and salt are dissolved. Add steaks to brine. Cover and refrigerate 12 hours or overnight.

Drain and discard brine from steaks. Rinse with water. Pat dry with paper towels. Arrange steaks on cooling racks. Air dry for 1 hour, or until steaks are shiny and dry.

Place oven thermometer in smoker. Heat dry smoker for 20 minutes, or until temperature registers 100°F. Spray smoker racks with nonstick vegetable cooking spray. Arrange steaks on prepared racks, spacing at least ½ inch apart.

Smoke steaks according to smoker manufacturer's directions (approximately 4 to 6 hours), or until fish is firm and opaque and internal temperature registers 180°F in thickest part of steak, adding wood chips as necessary to impart desired flavor and to maintain desired level of smoke. Store smoked fish, loosely wrapped, in refrigerator no longer than 2 weeks. Serve with thick slices of crusty French bread or crackers.

Per Serving: Calories: 159 • Protein: 20 g.
• Carbohydrate: 4 g. • Fat: 6 g.
• Cholesterol: 55 mg. • Sodium: 998 mg.
Exchanges: 3 lean meat

Tropical Smoked Salmon

Kathleen D. Bingman – Benicia, California

BRINE:

- 2 cups orange juice
- 1½ cups pineapple juice
- ½ cup water
- ½ cup packed brown sugar
- ¼ cup canning or pickling salt
- ¼ cup honey
- 3 tablespoons lemon juice
- 1 tablespoon lemon pepper
- 1 clove garlic, minced
- 1 lb. salmon, or substitute, fillets (8 oz. each), 1 inch thick, skin on

4 servings

In 5-quart glass or plastic container, combine brine ingredients. Stir until sugar and salt are dissolved. Add fillets to brine. Cover and refrigerate 12 hours or overnight.

Drain and discard brine from fillets. Rinse with water. Pat dry with paper towels. Arrange fillets on cooling racks. Air dry for 1 hour, or until fillets are shiny and dry.

Place oven thermometer in smoker. Heat dry smoker for 20 minutes, or until temperature registers 100°F. Spray smoker racks with nonstick vegetable cooking spray. Arrange fillets on prepared racks, spacing at least ½ inch apart.

Smoke fillets according to smoker manufacturer's directions (approximately 4 to 6 hours), or until fish is firm and opaque and internal temperature registers 180°F in thickest part of fillet, adding wood chips as necessary to impart desired flavor and to maintain desired level of smoke. Store smoked fish, loosely wrapped, in refrigerator no longer than 2 weeks. Serve with crackers.

Per Serving: Calories: 379 • Protein: 45 g.
• Carbohydrate: 14 g. • Fat: 14 g.
• Cholesterol: 125 mg. • Sodium: 1704 mg.
Exchanges: 7 lean meat, 1 fruit

Honey-glazed Smoked Salmon ↑

Jim Stacchiotti – Girard, Ohio

8 cups water
3/4 cup canning or pickling salt
1/3 cup packed brown sugar
1/2 teaspoon pepper
1/2 teaspoon onion powder

3 lbs. salmon, or substitute, fillets (8 oz. each), 1 inch thick, skin removed, cut into 3 × 4-inch pieces
1/2 cup margarine or butter, melted
1 cup honey

12 servings

In 5-quart glass or plastic container, combine water, salt, sugar, pepper and onion powder. Stir until salt and sugar are dissolved. Add salmon pieces to brine. Cover and refrigerate 8 hours or overnight.

Drain and discard brine from salmon. Rinse with water. Pat dry with paper towels. Arrange salmon pieces on cooling racks. Air dry for 1 hour, or until pieces are shiny and dry.

Heat oven to 350°F. Spray two 13 × 9-inch baking dishes with nonstick vegetable cooking spray. Arrange salmon pieces in single layer in each dish. In small mixing bowl, combine melted margarine and honey. Spoon honey mixture evenly over salmon in each dish. Bake for 20 to 30 minutes, or until fish is firm, basting once or twice. Cool slightly. Cover dishes with plastic wrap. Chill 3 hours.

Place oven thermometer in smoker. Heat dry smoker for 20 minutes, or until temperature registers 100°F. Spray smoker racks with nonstick vegetable cooking spray. Arrange salmon pieces on prepared racks, spacing at least 1/2 inch apart.

Smoke fillets according to smoker manufacturer's directions (approximately 1 1/2 to 3 hours), or until fish is firm and opaque and internal temperature registers 180°F in thickest part of fillet, adding wood chips as necessary to impart desired flavor and to maintain desired level of smoke. Store smoked fish, loosely wrapped, in refrigerator no longer than 2 weeks. Serve with crackers.

Per Serving: Calories: 243 • Protein: 23 g. • Carbohydrate: 13 g. • Fat: 11 g.
• Cholesterol: 62 mg. • Sodium: 894 mg.
Exchanges: 3 lean meat, 3/4 fruit, 1/2 fat

Marv's Guide Service Secret Smoked Fish Recipe

Marv McQuinn – Hillsboro, Oregon

BRINE:
4 cups water
2 cups soy sauce
2 cups apple juice
1 cup packed brown sugar
1/2 cup canning or pickling salt
2 tablespoons whole black peppercorns
1 teaspoon garlic powder
1 teaspoon onion powder
1 teaspoon freshly ground pepper

3 lbs. lake trout, or substitute, fillets (8 oz. each), 1 inch thick, skin on

12 servings

In 5-quart glass or plastic container, combine brine ingredients. Stir until sugar and salt are dissolved. Add fillets to brine. Cover and refrigerate 12 hours or overnight.

Drain and discard brine from fillets. Rinse with water. Pat dry with paper towels. Arrange fillets on cooling racks. Air dry for 1 hour, or until fillets are shiny and dry.

Place oven thermometer in smoker. Heat dry smoker for 20 minutes, or until temperature registers 100°F. Spray smoker racks with nonstick vegetable cooking spray. Arrange fillets on prepared racks, spacing at least 1/2 inch apart.

Smoke fillets according to smoker manufacturer's directions (approximately 6 to 8 hours), or until fish is firm and opaque and internal temperature registers 180°F in thickest part of fillet, adding wood chips as necessary to impart desired flavor and to maintain desired level of smoke. Store smoked fish, loosely wrapped, in refrigerator no longer than 2 weeks. Serve with crackers.

Per Serving: Calories: 185 • Protein: 24 g.
• Carbohydrate: 4 g. • Fat: 8 g.
• Cholesterol: 66 mg. • Sodium: 870 mg.
Exchanges: 3 lean meat, 1/4 fruit

Smoked Whitefish →

Robert C. Reed – Grover City, California

BRINE:

- 6 cups water
- ⅔ cup sugar
- ½ cup packed brown sugar
- ½ cup canning or pickling salt
- ⅓ cup soy sauce
- 2 cloves garlic, crushed
- 1 tablespoon pepper
- 2 bay leaves, crushed

- 2 lbs. whitefish, or substitute, fillets (8 oz. each), ½ inch thick, skin on

8 servings

In 5-quart glass or plastic container, combine brine ingredients. Stir until sugar and salt are dissolved. Add fillets to brine. Cover and refrigerate 12 hours or overnight.

Drain and discard brine from fillets. Rinse with water. Pat dry with paper towels. Arrange fillets on cooling racks. Air dry for 1 hour, or until fillets are shiny and dry.

Place oven thermometer in smoker. Heat dry smoker for 20 minutes, or until temperature registers 100°F. Spray smoker racks with nonstick vegetable cooking spray. Arrange fillets on prepared racks, spacing at least ½ inch apart.

Smoke fillets according to smoker manufacturer's directions (approximately 6 to 8 hours), or until fish is firm and opaque and internal temperature registers 180°F in thickest part of fillet, adding wood chips as necessary to impart desired flavor and to maintain desired level of smoke. Store smoked fish, loosely wrapped, in refrigerator no longer than 2 weeks. Serve with crackers.

Per Serving: Calories: 177 • Protein: 22 g.
• Carbohydrate: 6 g. • Fat: 7 g.
• Cholesterol: 68 mg. • Sodium: 940 mg.
Exchanges: 3 lean meat, ½ fruit

Cajun Smoked Trout

Marilyn Lawrence – North Little Rock, Arkansas

- 4 to 6 cups mesquite wood chips

SEASONINGS:
- 1 tablespoon Cavender's® Greek seasoning
- 1 tablespoon Cajun fish seasoning
- 1 teaspoon garlic powder
- ¼ teaspoon freshly ground pepper
- 1 cup vegetable oil
- 4 whole drawn stream trout (8 oz. each)

4 servings

Place wood chips in large mixing bowl. Cover with water. Soak chips for 1 hour. Place oven thermometer in smoker. Heat wet smoker with filled water pan for 20 minutes, or until temperature registers 100°F. Spray smoker racks with nonstick vegetable cooking spray. In small bowl, combine seasoning ingredients. Set aside.

Pour oil in 11 × 7-inch baking dish. Place trout in baking dish, turning to coat exterior and cavity liberally with oil. Remove trout from dish. Sprinkle both sides and cavity of each trout evenly with seasonings. Arrange trout on prepared racks, spacing at least ½ inch apart. Drain and discard water from wood chips.

Smoke trout with wet chips according to smoker manufacturer's directions (approximately 2 to 3 hours), or until fish flakes when fork is inserted at backbone in thickest part of fish and internal temperature registers 180°F in thickest part of fish. Serve hot as main dish, or cold as an appetizer.

Per Serving: Calories: 300 • Protein: 29 g. • Carbohydrate: 3 g. • Fat: 19 g.
• Cholesterol: 80 mg. • Sodium: 1329 mg.
Exchanges: ¼ starch, 4 lean meat, 1¼ fat

Capt. Andy's Sugar-smoked Walleye

Capt. Andy Emrisko – Cleveland, Ohio

BRINE:

8 cups apple juice

¾ cup canning or pickling salt

¼ cup packed brown sugar

3 lbs. walleye, salmon, or
substitute, fillets (8 oz. each),
½ to 1 inch thick, skin on

4 to 6 cups cherry wood chips

8 cups apple juice

¼ cup packed brown sugar

GLAZE:

½ cup apple juice

1 tablespoon packed brown sugar

1 teaspoon honey

12 servings

In 5-quart glass or plastic container, combine brine ingredients. Stir until salt and sugar are dissolved. Add fillets to brine. Cover and refrigerate 12 hours or overnight.

Place wood chips in large mixing bowl. Cover with water. Soak chips for 1 hour. Drain and discard brine from fillets. Rinse with water. Pat dry with paper towels. Arrange fillets on cooling racks. Air dry for 1 hour, or until fillets are shiny and dry.

Place oven thermometer in smoker. Add 8 cups apple juice and ¼ cup brown sugar to water pan in smoker. Heat wet smoker with filled water pan for 20 minutes, or until temperature registers 100°F. Spray smoker racks with nonstick vegetable cooking spray. Arrange fillets on prepared racks, spacing at least ½ inch apart. Drain and discard water from wood chips.

Smoke fillets with wet chips according to smoker manufacturer's directions (approximately 2 to 3 hours), or until fish flakes easily with fork and internal temperature registers 180°F in thickest part of fillet.

In 1-quart saucepan, combine glaze ingredients. Cook over medium heat for 2 to 3 minutes, or until mixture is hot and sugar is dissolved, stirring frequently. Brush glaze over fillets. Continue smoking for 30 minutes to 1 hour, or until glaze is set. Store smoked fish, loosely wrapped, in refrigerator no longer than 2 weeks. Serve cold as an appetizer, or hot as a main dish.

Per Serving: Calories: 134 • Protein: 22 g. • Carbohydrate: 8 g. • Fat: 2 g.
• Cholesterol: 98 mg. • Sodium: 943 mg.
Exchanges: 3 lean meat, ½ fruit

140

Water-smoked Barbecued Lake Trout

"Great appetizer, warm or chilled!"
Gregory Sutkus – Hickory Hills, Illinois

BRINE:

    8 cups water
    ¾ cup canning or pickling salt
    ¾ cup packed brown sugar
    ½ cup barbecue sauce
  1½ teaspoons white pepper
    1 bay leaf

    6 lake trout, or substitute, steaks
       (8 oz. each), 1 inch thick
    4 to 6 cups cherry or apple wood
       chips

12 servings

In 4-quart saucepan, combine brine ingredients. Bring to a rolling boil over high heat, stirring constantly to dissolve salt and sugar. Remove from heat. Cool completely. Place lake trout steaks in 5-quart glass or plastic container. Pour brine over steaks. Cover and chill 4 hours.

Place wood chips in large mixing bowl. Cover with water. Soak chips for 1 hour. Drain and discard brine from steaks. Rinse with water. Pat dry with paper towels. Arrange steaks on cooling racks. Air dry for 1 hour, or until steaks are shiny and dry.

Place oven thermometer in smoker. Heat wet smoker with filled water pan for 20 minutes, or until temperature registers 100°F. Spray smoker racks with nonstick vegetable cooking spray. Arrange steaks on prepared racks, spacing at least ½ inch apart. Drain and discard water from wood chips. Smoke fish with wet chips according to smoker manufacturer's directions (approximately 2 to 3 hours), or until fish flakes easily with fork and internal temperature registers 180°F in thickest part of steak. Serve cold as an appetizer, or hot as a main dish.

Per Serving: Calories: 157 • Protein: 21 g.
• Carbohydrate: 2 g. • Fat: 7 g.
• Cholesterol: 58 mg. • Sodium: 774 mg.
Exchanges: 3 lean meat, ¼ fruit

Water-smoked Perch & Bacon Bundles ↑

"Just eat them right off toothpicks. They make great appetizers or snacks."
Arthur M. Panfil – Garfield Heights, Ohio

BRINE:

    4 cups water
    2 tablespoons packed brown sugar
    2 tablespoons canning or pickling
       salt
    1 small bay leaf
    ¾ teaspoon ground cinnamon
    ¼ teaspoon pepper
    ¼ teaspoon garlic salt

    ¼ teaspoon onion salt
    ¼ teaspoon red pepper sauce

    1 lb. yellow perch, or substitute,
       fillets, skin removed, cut into
       4 × ¾ × ¼-inch strips (about
       36 strips)
    4 to 6 cups hickory wood chips
   18 strips bacon, cut in half crosswise
       Paprika
    4 cups water
    2 cups white wine

12 servings

In 2-quart saucepan, combine brine ingredients. Bring to a rolling boil over high heat. Reduce heat to low, and let brine simmer, partially covered, for 30 minutes. Remove from heat. Cool completely. Place perch strips in 2-quart glass or plastic container. Pour brine over strips. Cover and refrigerate 12 hours or overnight.

Place wood chips in large mixing bowl. Cover with water. Soak for 1 hour. Drain and discard brine from strips. Rinse with water. Pat dry with paper towels. Arrange strips on cooling racks. Air dry for 1 hour, or until strips are shiny and dry. In 10-inch skillet, fry bacon pieces over low heat for 5 to 8 minutes, or until lightly browned but not crisp. Place on paper-towel-lined plate to drain. Place 1 strip of fish on each bacon piece. Roll up and secure with wooden picks. Sprinkle bundles with paprika.

Place oven thermometer in smoker. Add 4 cups water and the wine to water pan in smoker. Heat wet smoker with filled water pan for 20 minutes, or until temperature registers 100°F. Spray smoker racks with nonstick vegetable cooking spray. Arrange bundles on prepared racks, spacing at least ½ inch apart. Drain and discard water from wood chips. Smoke bundles with wet chips according to smoker manufacturer's directions (approximately 2 to 3 hours), or until fish is firm and opaque, turning bundles over once.

Per Serving: Calories: 92 • Protein: 10 g. • Carbohydrate: 1 g. • Fat: 5 g.
• Cholesterol: 42 mg. • Sodium: 390 mg.
Exchanges: 1½ lean meat

Smoked Salmon, Tomato & Leek Tart

Darina Allen – Ballymaloe Cookery School, Shanagarry, Co. Cork, Ireland

SHORTCRUST PASTRY:*

¾ cup plus 2 tablespoons
    all-purpose flour
¼ cup cold butter, cut into ½-inch dice
1 egg, beaten

FILLING:

2 tablespoons butter, divided
½ lb. very ripe tomatoes, peeled,
    seeded and diced (1⅓ cups)
    Dash sugar
3 cups thinly sliced leeks
¼ cup dry white wine
½ cup heavy cream, divided
¼ cup milk
1 egg
1 egg yolk
    Pinch of Hungarian paprika
5 oz. smoked salmon, or
    substitute, sliced into
    ⅛-inch slices, then cut into
    ¼-inch strips
1 teaspoon snipped fresh dill
    weed

6 servings

Heat oven to 375°F. Sift flour into medium mixing bowl. Add ¼ cup diced butter. Rub butter into flour, using fingertips, until particles are of uniform size. Add beaten egg gradually, mixing with fork until particles are moistened and cling together. Form dough into ball. Cover with plastic wrap. Chill 30 minutes.

On lightly floured board, roll dough out at least 2 inches larger than 9-inch tart pan. Ease dough into tart pan. Trim edges. Cut 9-inch circle of parchment paper. Line tart pan with paper. Fill with dried beans or pie weights. Blind-bake crust for 20 to 25 minutes, or until lightly browned. Remove and discard dried beans and paper. Set crust aside. Reduce oven temperature to 350°F.

Place 1 tablespoon butter in 8-inch skillet. Melt butter over medium-high heat. Add tomatoes and sugar. Season to taste with salt and freshly ground pepper. Cook for 2 to 3 minutes, or until tomatoes soften, stirring frequently. Remove from heat. Set aside.

Melt remaining 1 tablespoon butter in 1-quart saucepan over medium heat. Add leeks; toss to coat. Reduce heat to low. Cover. Cook for 8 to 10 minutes, or until leeks are tender, stirring frequently. Add wine. Simmer for 2 to 3 minutes. Add ¼ cup cream. Simmer gently for 8 to 10 minutes, or until cream is almost absorbed. Remove from heat. Season to taste with salt and freshly ground pepper. Set aside.

Place remaining ¼ cup cream, the milk, egg, egg yolk and paprika in medium mixing bowl. Beat together. Season with salt and freshly ground pepper. Add tomatoes, leeks, salmon and dill. Spoon mixture into prebaked crust. Bake for 30 to 35 minutes, or until mixture is set and golden brown on top.

* Substitute one prerolled refrigerated piecrust for shortcrust pastry, if desired.

Per Serving: Calories: 343 • Protein: 11 g. • Carbohydrate: 24 g. • Fat: 23 g.
• Cholesterol: 171 mg. • Sodium: 351 mg.
Exchanges: 1 starch, 1 lean meat, ½ fruit, 4 fat

Smoked Salmon Triangles →

Ruth Holcomb – Spring Lake, North Carolina

½ cup margarine or butter, softened
2 tablespoons snipped fresh chives
1 tablespoon prepared horseradish
¼ teaspoon garlic powder
¼ teaspoon salt
8 slices dark rye or whole wheat bread
6 to 8 oz. smoked salmon, or substitute, flaked (1¼ cups)
1 small tomato, cut into 8 thin slices
  Coarsely ground fresh pepper
8 sprigs fresh dill weed

8 servings

In small mixing bowl, combine margarine, chives, horseradish, garlic powder and salt. Spread about 1 tablespoon margarine mixture evenly on each slice of bread. Trim crusts from bread slices. Cut each slice in half diagonally to form triangles. Top each triangle evenly with flaked salmon. Cut tomato slices in half and place 1 half slice on each triangle. Sprinkle evenly with pepper. Garnish each triangle with sprig of dill.

Per Serving: Calories: 202 • Protein: 8 g.
• Carbohydrate: 15 g. • Fat: 13 g.
• Cholesterol: 6 mg. • Sodium: 543 mg.
Exchanges: 1 starch, ⅔ lean meat, 2 fat

Spinach Pasta with Smoked Bass & Cream Sauce

Annette Bignami – Moscow, Idaho

16 oz. uncooked spinach egg noodles
3 tablespoons margarine or butter, divided
2 cups heavy cream
1 to 3 teaspoons freshly ground pepper
1 teaspoon salt
3 tablespoons grated Parmesan cheese
5 oz. smoked bass, or substitute, flaked (1 cup)
⅓ cup snipped fresh dill weed

6 to 8 servings

Prepare noodles as directed on package. Rinse and drain. Place in large mixing bowl or serving bowl. Add 1 tablespoon plus 1½ teaspoons margarine. Toss to coat. Cover to keep warm. Set aside.

In 1-quart saucepan, combine cream and remaining 1 tablespoon plus 1½ teaspoons margarine. Cook, stirring constantly over low heat, until mixture begins to simmer. Add pepper and salt. Cook for 15 to 20 minutes, or until cream mixture is reduced by one-third, stirring frequently.

Stir in Parmesan cheese, bass and dill. Cook for 2 to 3 minutes, or until hot, stirring frequently. Add cream sauce to noodles. Toss to coat. Serve immediately. Serve with additional Parmesan cheese, if desired.

Nutritional information not available.

Smoked Trout Salad

Richard J. Parmley – St. Louis, Missouri

16 oz. uncooked rotini
6 cups water
1 medium red onion, cut into thin wedges
1 small zucchini, thinly sliced (½ cup)
½ cup fresh broccoli flowerets
2 smoked stream trout (8 oz. each),
  flaked (1¾ cups)
1 large red pepper, cut into 2 × ¼-inch strips
  (1½ cups)
½ cup salad dressing or mayonnaise
3 tablespoons fresh lemon juice
3 tablespoons drained capers
2 tablespoons thinly sliced green onion
1 teaspoon snipped fresh parsley
½ teaspoon salt
¼ teaspoon pepper

6 to 8 servings

Prepare rotini as directed on package. Rinse and drain. Place in large mixing bowl or salad bowl. Cover with plastic wrap. Set aside.

In 3-quart saucepan, bring water to a simmer over medium-high heat. Fill large mixing bowl with ice water. Set aside.

Plunge onion wedges into simmering water for 15 to 30 seconds, or just until color brightens. Lift from simmering water with slotted spoon. Plunge immediately into ice water.

Repeat with zucchini and broccoli. Drain vegetables. Add to rotini. Add remaining ingredients. Mix well. Cover with plastic wrap. Chill 1 hour.

Per Serving: Calories: 310 • Protein: 13 g. • Carbohydrate: 49 g. • Fat: 7 g. • Cholesterol: 10 mg. • Sodium: 534 mg.
Exchanges: 2¾ starch, 1 medium-fat meat, 1½ vegetable

Mousse de Saumon Fumé

Frederick W. Montanye –
Chateau de Saussignac Cooking School, Saussignac, France

10 oz. smoked salmon, or substitute, flaked (2 cups)
¾ cup heavy cream
¼ cup plus 2 tablespoons margarine or butter, softened
¾ teaspoon prepared horseradish

GARNISH:
6 sage leaves
1 small red or yellow pepper, cut into 12 diamonds (½ inch wide at points)
  Lumpfish caviar (optional)

6 servings

In food processor or blender, process salmon, cream, margarine and horseradish until smooth. Spoon mixture evenly into six 4-oz. ramequins, packing lightly. Using back of spoon, smooth top of each mousse. Place 1 sage leaf in center of each ramequin. Arrange 2 pepper diamonds with points touching at base of sage leaf. Place small dollop of caviar above point where diamonds touch. Serve as first course with toast rounds or crackers.

Variation: Substitute finely chopped black olives for caviar, if desired.

Per Serving: Calories: 265 • Protein: 10 g. • Carbohydrate: 2 g.
• Fat: 25 g. • Cholesterol: 52 mg. • Sodium: 535 mg.
Exchanges: 1¼ lean meat, 4 fat

Garlic-smoked Whitefish Spread

John Holt – Whitefish, Montana

5 oz. smoked whitefish, or substitute, flaked (1 cup)
1 pkg. (8 oz.) cream cheese, softened
¼ cup sour cream
½ teaspoon lime juice
⅛ teaspoon freshly ground pepper
⅛ teaspoon salt
⅛ teaspoon cayenne
1 clove garlic, minced
¼ cup pimiento-stuffed green olives, sliced

2 cups, 16 servings

In medium mixing bowl, combine fish, cream cheese and sour cream. Add remaining ingredients, except olives. Gently stir in olive slices. Cover with plastic wrap. Chill at least 1 hour. Serve with crackers or crisp bread sticks.

Per Serving: Calories: 71 • Protein: 4 g. • Carbohydrate: 1 g.
• Fat: 6 g. • Cholesterol: 21 mg. • Sodium: 221 mg.
Exchanges: ½ lean meat, 1 fat

Pickling

Techniques for Pickling

Pickled fish is usually the first item to disappear from the appetizer tray. Most people like to eat it with crackers.

Practically any kind of fish can be pickled, but small fish with delicate flesh generally work better than large fish with coarse meat. Bony fish, such as northern pike, are often pickled because the acid in the pickling liquid helps dissolve the small bones.

There are dozens of different pickling techniques. Generally, the fish is soaked in a vinegar-salt brine and then in a pickling liquid consisting of vinegar, sugar and seasonings. Total brining and pickling time varies from 4 to 20 days, depending on the recipe.

Normally, the fish are packed in canning jars (with two-part sealing lids) along with spices and onions.

Seviche is another popular appetizer made by marinating uncooked fish in citrus juice and adding onions, tomatoes, peppers and spices.

Fresh, uncooked fish should be frozen for at least 48 hours before pickling, in case the meat contains tapeworms. Seldom is this a problem, but the broad-fish tapeworm, found mainly in Canada, can be transmitted to humans and produce symptoms much like intestinal flu. If a recipe recommends cooking the fish in the brine, there is no need to freeze the meat first.

Pickled fish can be stored in the refrigerator for up to 4 weeks. Seviche is best when eaten fresh.

Tips for Pickling Fish

USE soft or distilled water with canning or pickling salt for brining. The minerals in hard water and ordinary table salt (inset) result in off flavors and colors.

KEEP fish submerged in the brine by placing a plate over the fish and a heavy object on the plate. This ensures that all the fish is pickled.

MAKE "cream-style" pickled fish by draining off the brine before serving, then adding a sour cream and sugar mixture (1 tablespoon sugar to 1 cup sour cream).

Trout Seviche

Norm and Sil Strung – Bozeman, Montana

1 lb. stream trout, or substitute, fillets (2 oz. each), skin removed
1 cup fresh key lime juice
¼ cup minced jalapeño peppers
4 medium tomatoes, seeded and chopped (4 cups)
1 cup finely chopped red onion
1 cup thinly sliced celery
¼ cup halved pimiento-stuffed green olives
1 teaspoon freshly ground black pepper
1 teaspoon salt

16 servings

Freeze fish 48 hours at 0°F. Defrost. Cut into ½-inch pieces. Place fish in large glass or plastic bowl. Add juice and jalapeño peppers. Mix well. Add remaining ingredients, except salt, stirring gently to combine. With back of spoon, gently press mixture down into juices. Sprinkle salt evenly over top. Cover with plastic wrap. Chill 1 hour. Serve on toasted tortilla bits or crackers. Store in refrigerator no longer than 1 to 2 days.

Per Serving: Calories: 56 • Protein: 7 g. • Carbohydrate: 5 g. • Fat: 1 g. • Cholesterol: 16 mg. • Sodium: 208 mg.
Exchanges: ¾ lean meat, 1 vegetable

Pickled Jacks

"This is a recipe my husband brought home from Chantrey Inlet Lodge in the Arctic Circle."
Betty R. White – Polo, Illinois

3 lbs. northern pike, or substitute, fillets (4 to 6 oz. each), skin removed
4 cups water
1 cup canning or pickling salt
8 cups distilled white vinegar, divided
1 large red or white onion, thinly sliced
2½ cups sugar
1 tablespoon plus 1 teaspoon mustard seed
6 bay leaves
10 whole cloves

3 quarts

Freeze fish 48 hours at 0°F. Defrost. Cut into ½-inch strips. In large glass mixing bowl, combine water and salt. Stir until salt is almost dissolved. Add fish. Cover with plastic wrap. Refrigerate 2 days. Drain and discard brine. Rinse fish in cold water until rinse water is clear. Drain.

In same bowl, place fish and 4 cups vinegar. Cover with plastic wrap. Refrigerate 1 day. Drain and discard vinegar. Do not rinse fish. In three 1-quart jars, loosely layer fish and onion. Cover and chill.

In 2-quart saucepan, combine remaining 4 cups vinegar, the sugar and remaining ingredients. Bring mixture to a boil over medium-high heat, stirring constantly until sugar is dissolved. Reduce heat to medium-low and simmer for 15 minutes. Remove from heat. Cool completely. Pour pickling liquid over fish to cover. Seal jars, using two-part sealing lids. Refrigerate 1 week before serving. Store in refrigerator no longer than 4 weeks.

Nutritional information not available.

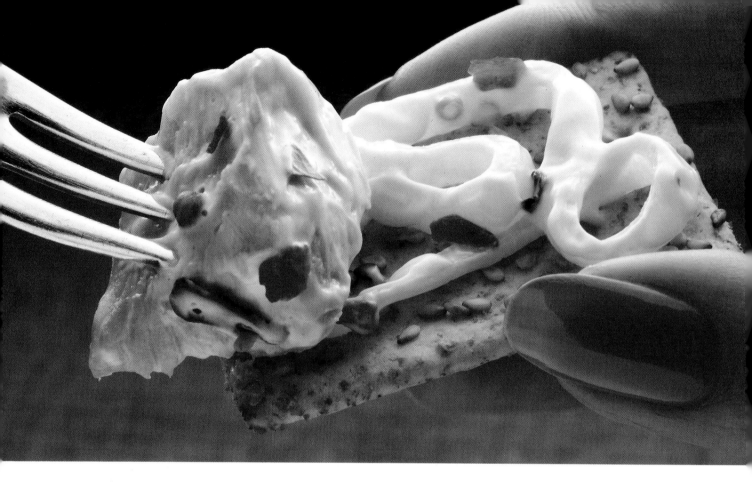

Creamed Salmon ↑

Lynn E. DeWitt – West Olive, Michigan

3½ lbs. salmon, or substitute, fillets (8 oz. each), skin removed
3 to 4 medium onions, sliced
4 cups distilled white vinegar
2 cups plus 2 tablespoons sugar, divided
¼ cup mixed pickling spices
½ cup canning or pickling salt
1 carton (16 oz.) sour cream

3 quarts

Freeze fish 48 hours at 0°F. Defrost. Cut into 1 to 2-inch pieces. Set aside. In large glass mixing bowl, combine onions, vinegar, 2 cups sugar, the spices and salt. Stir until sugar and salt are almost dissolved.

Add fish. Cover with plastic wrap. Refrigerate 7 days, stirring mixture once every day. Drain and discard brine, reserving fish, onions and spices.

In large mixing bowl, combine sour cream and remaining 2 tablespoons sugar. Add fish mixture. Stir gently to coat. Loosely pack mixture into three 1-quart jars. Seal jars, using two-part sealing lids. Store in refrigerator no longer than 4 weeks.

Nutritional information not available.

Pickled Whitefish

Jerry L. Smalley – Columbia Falls, Montana

2 to 3 lbs. whitefish, or substitute, fillets (4 to 6 oz. each), skin removed
8 cups distilled white vinegar, divided
1 cup canning or pickling salt
1 large white onion, sliced
3 cups sugar
1 cup white wine
¼ cup mixed pickling spices

3 quarts

Freeze fish 48 hours at 0°F. Defrost. Cut into 1 to 2-inch pieces. Set aside. In large glass mixing bowl, combine 4 cups vinegar and the salt. Stir until salt is almost dissolved. Add fish. Cover with plastic wrap. Refrigerate 5 days. Drain and discard brine. Rinse fish in cold water until rinse water is clear. Drain.

In three 1-quart jars, loosely layer fish and onion. Cover and chill. In 3-quart saucepan, combine remaining 4 cups vinegar, the sugar, wine and spices. Bring mixture to a boil over medium-high heat, stirring constantly until sugar is dissolved. Remove from heat. Cool completely. Pour pickling liquid over fish to cover. Seal jars, using two-part sealing lids. Refrigerate 4 days before serving, inverting jar each day to mix contents. Store in refrigerator no longer than 4 weeks.

Nutritional information not available.

Easy Pickled Northern

"Mother's recipe."
James H. Wright – Mt. Holly, New Jersey

1½ lbs. northern pike, or substitute,
      fillets (4 to 6 oz. each), skin
      removed, cut into 2 to 3-inch
      pieces
1   tablespoon plus 1½ teaspoons
      mixed pickling spices
1   medium red onion, thinly sliced
3   slices lemon
1   quart distilled white vinegar
2   cups sugar

3 pints

Heat oven to 325°F. Arrange fish in single layer in 13 × 9-inch baking dish. Sprinkle pickling spices evenly over fish. Top with onion and lemon slices. Pour vinegar over fish. Bake for 1 hour. Cool slightly. Cover with plastic wrap. Chill 4 hours, or until cold.

With slotted spoon, remove fish and onion from vinegar. Reserve vinegar. In three 1-pint jars, loosely layer fish and onion. Cover and chill. In 2-quart saucepan, combine reserved vinegar and the sugar. Bring mixture to a boil over medium-high heat, stirring constantly until sugar is dissolved.

Pour pickling liquid over fish to cover. Seal jars, using two-part sealing lids. Chill. Store in refrigerator no longer than 4 weeks.

Nutritional information not available.

Peppercorn Fish Pickles

Fred Kakac – Marengo, Illinois

6	lbs. northern pike, or substitute, fillets (4 to 6 oz. each), skin removed
2	gallons water, divided
3½	cups canning or pickling salt, divided
11	cups distilled white vinegar, divided
1	large onion, thinly sliced
4½	cups sugar
2	tablespoons mustard seed
6	bay leaves
3	teaspoons whole cloves
1	to 2 tablespoons whole black, red or green peppercorns

4 quarts, 1 pint

Freeze fish 48 hours at 0°F. Defrost. Cut into 1 to 2-inch pieces. Set aside. In large glass mixing bowl, combine 1 gallon water and 1 cup salt. Stir until salt is almost dissolved. Add fish. Soak for 1 hour. Drain and discard brine.

In another large glass bowl, combine remaining 1 gallon water and 2½ cups salt. Stir until salt is almost dissolved. Add fish. Cover with plastic wrap. Refrigerate 12 hours. Drain and discard brine. Rinse fish with cold water until rinse water is clear. In same bowl, pour 5 cups vinegar over fish. Cover with plastic wrap. Refrigerate 2 days. Drain and discard vinegar.

In four 1-quart jars and one 1-pint jar, loosely layer fish and onion. Cover and chill. In 4-quart saucepan, combine remaining 6 cups vinegar and remaining ingredients. Bring mixture to a boil over medium-high heat. Boil for 5 minutes. Cool completely. Pour pickling liquid over fish to cover. Seal jars, using two-part sealing lids. Refrigerate 2 to 3 days before serving. Store in refrigerator no longer than 4 weeks.

Nutritional information not available.

Pickled Fish

Keith Sutton – Benton, Arkansas

3 lbs. any freshwater fish fillets (4 to 6 oz. each), skin removed
4 cups water
1 cup canning or pickling salt
9 cups distilled white vinegar, divided
1 large red or white onion, thinly sliced
2½ cups sugar
5 bay leaves
¼ cup plus 1 tablespoon mixed pickling spices
¼ cup bottled lemon juice

3 quarts

Freeze fish 48 hours at 0°F. Defrost. Cut into 1 to 2-inch pieces. Set aside. In large glass mixing bowl, combine water and salt. Stir until salt is almost dissolved. Add fish. Cover with plastic wrap. Refrigerate 2 days. Drain and discard brine. Rinse fish in cold water until rinse water is clear. Drain.

In same bowl, place fish and 4 cups vinegar. Cover with plastic wrap. Refrigerate 2 days. Drain and discard vinegar. Rinse fish in cold water until rinse water is clear. Drain.

In three 1-quart jars, loosely layer fish and onion. Cover and chill.

In 2-quart saucepan, combine remaining 5 cups vinegar, the sugar, bay leaves and pickling spices. Bring mixture to a boil over medium-high heat, stirring constantly until sugar is dissolved. Remove from heat. Cool completely. Stir in juice. Pour pickling liquid over fish to cover. Seal jars, using two-part sealing lids. Refrigerate 4 to 5 days before serving. Store in refrigerator no longer than 4 weeks.

Nutritional information not available.

Sweet Pepper Pickled Fish ↑

Thomas K. Squier – Aberdeen, North Carolina

2 to 3 lbs. any freshwater fish fillets (4 to 6 oz. each), skin removed
8 cups apple cider vinegar
¼ cup canning or pickling salt
1½ cups sugar
3 tablespoons mixed pickling spices
½ cup chopped red pepper
1 large white onion, sliced

2 quarts

Freeze fish 48 hours at 0°F. Defrost. Cut into 1 to 2-inch pieces. Set aside. In large glass mixing bowl, combine vinegar and salt. Stir until salt is almost dissolved. Add fish. Cover with plastic wrap. Refrigerate 2 days.

With slotted spoon, remove fish from brine. Rinse fish with cold water until rinse water is clear. Reserve 3 cups brine. Cover and chill fish. Pour reserved brine into 4-quart saucepan. Add sugar, spices and red pepper. Bring mixture to a boil over medium-high heat, stirring constantly until sugar is dissolved. Remove from heat. Cool completely.

In two 1-quart jars, loosely layer fish and onion. Pour pickling liquid over fish to cover. Seal jars, using two-part sealing lids. Refrigerate 1 week before serving. Store in refrigerator no longer than 4 weeks.

Nutritional information not available.

Cousin Bruce's Pickled Salmon →

Ron Cotterman – Eagle River, Alaska

2 lbs. salmon, or substitute, fillets (8 oz. each), skin removed
¾ cup canning or pickling salt
1 cup apple cider vinegar
2 cups distilled white vinegar
2 cups sugar
¼ cup mixed pickling spices
4 to 5 thin slices lemon
¾ cup dry white wine
½ medium onion, sliced

2 quarts

Freeze fish 48 hours at 0°F. Defrost. Cut into 1 to 2-inch pieces. Place fish in large glass mixing bowl. Set aside. In medium mixing bowl, combine salt and cider vinegar. Stir until salt is almost dissolved. Pour over fish. Refrigerate 8 to 10 days, stirring every few days.

Drain and discard brine. Rinse fish in cold water until rinse water is clear. Cover with cold water. Chill 2 hours.

In 2-quart saucepan, combine white vinegar, sugar, spices and lemon slices. Heat mixture over medium heat, stirring constantly until sugar is dissolved. Do not boil. Remove from heat. Cool completely. Add wine.

Drain and discard water from fish. In two 1-quart jars, loosely layer fish and onion. Pour pickling liquid over fish to cover. Seal jars, using two-part sealing lids. Refrigerate 10 days before serving. Store in refrigerator no longer than 4 weeks.

Nutritional information not available.

Pisik's Pickled Pike

Barbara R. Pisik – Lincolnshire, Illinois

3 cups water, divided
3 cups distilled white vinegar, divided
2 tablespoons plus 1½ teaspoons canning or pickling salt, divided
½ teaspoon whole black peppercorns, divided
20 whole allspice, divided
2½ teaspoons celery seed, divided

8 bay leaves, divided
1¼ teaspoons mustard seed, divided
5 whole cloves, divided
2 small onions, thinly sliced
3 lbs. northern pike, or substitute, fillets (4 to 6 oz. each), skin removed
½ cup sugar

2 quarts

In 4-quart saucepan, combine 1 cup water, 1 cup vinegar, 1 tablespoon salt, ¼ teaspoon peppercorns, 8 allspice, 1 teaspoon celery seed, 3 bay leaves, ½ teaspoon mustard seed, 2 cloves and the onions. Bring mixture to a boil over medium heat. Boil for 10 minutes. Add fish. Reduce heat to low. Cook for 30 minutes, turning fish over once.

Remove from heat. Cool slightly. Drain and discard brine, reserving fish and onions. Place in single layer in flat pan. Cover with plastic wrap. Chill 2 hours, or until cold.

Cut fish into 1 to 2-inch pieces. In two 1-quart jars, loosely layer fish and onions. Cover and chill.

In 2-quart saucepan, combine remaining 2 cups water, 2 cups vinegar, 1 tablespoon plus 1½ teaspoons salt, ¼ teaspoon peppercorns, 12 allspice, 1½ teaspoons celery seed, 5 bay leaves, ¾ teaspoon mustard seed, 3 cloves and the sugar. Bring mixture to a boil over medium-high heat, stirring constantly until sugar is dissolved.

Remove from heat. Cool slightly. Pour pickling liquid over fish to cover. Seal jars, using two-part sealing lids. Chill. Store in refrigerator no longer than 4 weeks.

Nutritional information not available.

Hot Pepper Pickled Fish →

Audrey Spear – Mankato, Minnesota

3½ lbs. any freshwater fish fillets (4 to 6 oz. each), skin removed
1 medium onion, thinly sliced
5 small whole dried hot chilies
2 cups distilled white vinegar
1 cup sugar
¾ cup rosé wine
¼ cup canning or pickling salt
1 tablespoon mixed pickling spices

2 quarts, 1 pint

Freeze fish 48 hours at 0°F. Defrost. Cut into 1 to 2-inch pieces. In two 1-quart jars and one 1-pint jar, loosely layer fish, onion and chilies. Cover and chill.

In 2-quart saucepan, combine remaining ingredients. Bring mixture to a boil over medium-high heat, stirring constantly until sugar is dissolved. Remove from heat. Cool completely. Pour pickling liquid over fish to cover. Seal jars, using two-part sealing lids. Refrigerate 10 days before serving. Store in refrigerator no longer than 4 weeks.

Nutritional information not available.

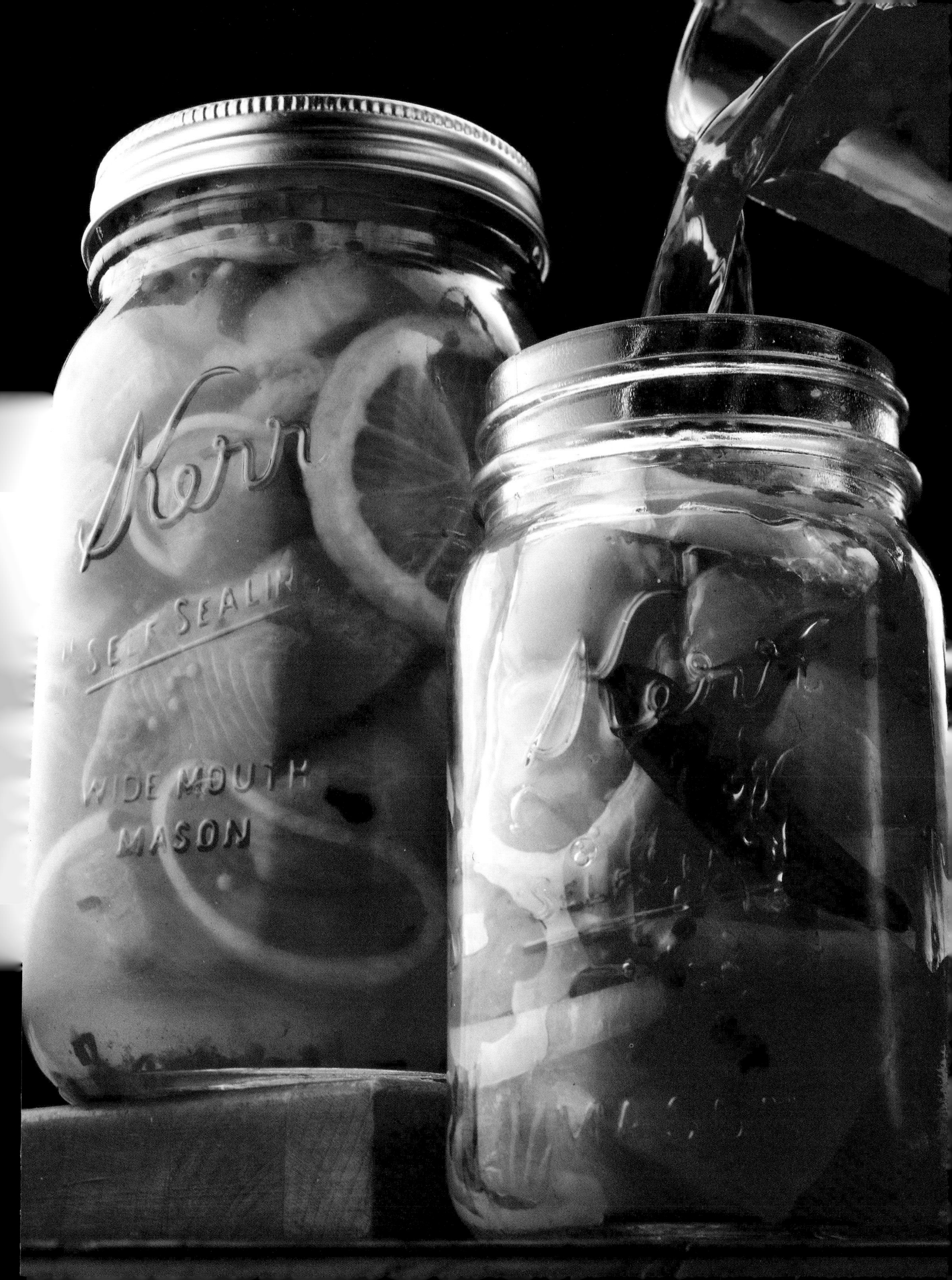
Kerr
WIDE MOUTH
MASON

Index

Creative Publishing international, Inc. offers
a variety of how-to books.
For information write:

Creative Publishing international, Inc.
Subscriber books
5900 Green Oak Drive
Minnetonka, MN 55343